INTRODUCING
ISSUES WITH
OPPOSING
VIEWPOINTS®

Stem Cell Research

Lauri S. Scherer, *Book Editor*

GREENHAVEN PRESS
A part of Gale, Cengage Learning

GALE
CENGAGE Learning·

Detroit • New York • San Francisco • New Haven, Conn • Waterville, Maine • London

Elizabeth Des Chenes, *Director, Publishing Solutions*

For more information, contact:
Greenhaven Press
27500 Drake Rd.
Farmington Hills, MI 48331-3535
Or you can visit our Internet site at gale.cengage.com

For product information and technology assistance, contact us at

Gale Customer Support, 1-800-877-4253
For permission to use material from this text or product, submit all requests online at
www.cengage.com/permissions

Further permissions questions can be e-mailed to permissionrequest@cengage.com

Articles in Greenhaven Press anthologies are often edited for length to meet page requirements. In addition, original titles of these works are changed to clearly present the main thesis and to explicitly indicate the author's opinion. Every effort is made to ensure that Greenhaven Press accurately reflects the original intent of the authors. Every effort has been made to trace the owners of copyrighted material.

Cover image © Creations/Shutterstock.com.

LIBRARY OF CONGRESS CATALOGING-IN-PUBLICATION DATA
Stem cell research / Lauri S. Scherer, book editor.
p. cm. -- (Introducing issues with opposing viewpoints)
Includes bibliographical references and index.
ISBN 978-0-7377-6282-2 (hardcover)
1. Stem cells--Research--United States. 2. Stem cells--Social aspects--United States.
I. Scherer, Lauri S.
QH588.S83S73935 2012
174.2'8--dc23
2012013994

Printed in the United States of America
1 2 3 4 5 6 7 16 15 14 13 12

Contents

Chapter 3: To What Extent Should the Government Support Stem Cell Research?

Foreword

I ndulging in a wide spectrum of ideas, beliefs, and perspectives is a critical cornerstone of democracy. After all, it is often debates over differences of opinion, such as whether to legalize abortion, how to treat prisoners, or when to enact the death penalty, that shape our society and drive it forward. Such diversity of thought is frequently regarded as the hallmark of a healthy and civilized culture. As the Reverend Clifford Schutjer of the First Congregational Church in Mansfield, Ohio, declared in a 2001 sermon, "Surrounding oneself with only like-minded people, restricting what we listen to or read only to what we find agreeable is irresponsible. Refusing to entertain doubts once we make up our minds is a subtle but deadly form of arrogance." With this advice in mind, Introducing Issues with Opposing Viewpoints books aim to open readers' minds to the critically divergent views that comprise our world's most important debates.

Introducing Issues with Opposing Viewpoints simplifies for students the enormous and often overwhelming mass of material now available via print and electronic media. Collected in every volume is an array of opinions that captures the essence of a particular controversy or topic. Introducing Issues with Opposing Viewpoints books embody the spirit of nineteenth-century journalist Charles A. Dana's axiom: "Fight for your opinions, but do not believe that they contain the whole truth, or the only truth." Absorbing such contrasting opinions teaches students to analyze the strength of an argument and compare it to its opposition. From this process readers can inform and strengthen their own opinions, or be exposed to new information that will change their minds. Introducing Issues with Opposing Viewpoints is a mosaic of different voices. The authors are statesmen, pundits, academics, journalists, corporations, and ordinary people who have felt compelled to share their experiences and ideas in a public forum. Their words have been collected from newspapers, journals, books, speeches, interviews, and the Internet, the fastest growing body of opinionated material in the world.

Introducing Issues with Opposing Viewpoints shares many of the well-known features of its critically acclaimed parent series, Opposing Viewpoints. The articles are presented in a pro/con format, allowing readers to absorb divergent perspectives side by side. Active reading questions preface each viewpoint, requiring the student to approach the material thoughtfully and carefully. Useful charts, graphs, and cartoons supplement each article. A thorough introduction provides readers with crucial background on an issue. An annotated bibliography points the reader toward articles, books, and websites that contain additional information on the topic. An appendix of organizations to contact contains a wide variety of charities, nonprofit organizations, political groups, and private enterprises that each hold a position on the issue at hand. Finally, a comprehensive index allows readers to locate content quickly and efficiently.

Introducing Issues with Opposing Viewpoints is also significantly different from Opposing Viewpoints. As the series title implies, its presentation will help introduce students to the concept of opposing viewpoints and learn to use this material to aid in critical writing and debate. The series' four-color, accessible format makes the books attractive and inviting to readers of all levels. In addition, each viewpoint has been carefully edited to maximize a reader's understanding of the content. Short but thorough viewpoints capture the essence of an argument. A substantial, thought-provoking essay question placed at the end of each viewpoint asks the student to further investigate the issues raised in the viewpoint, compare and contrast two authors' arguments, or consider how one might go about forming an opinion on the topic at hand. Each viewpoint contains sidebars that include at-a-glance information and handy statistics. A Facts About section located in the back of the book further supplies students with relevant facts and figures.

Following in the tradition of the Opposing Viewpoints series, Greenhaven Press continues to provide readers with invaluable exposure to the controversial issues that shape our world. As John Stuart Mill once wrote: "The only way in which a human being can make some approach to knowing the whole of a subject is by hearing what can be said about it by persons of every variety of opinion and studying all modes in which it can be looked at by every character of mind. No wise man ever acquired his wisdom in any mode but this." It is to this principle that Introducing Issues with Opposing Viewpoints books are dedicated.

Introduction

Nine-year-old Kara Anderson, of Chicago, suffers from cerebral palsy, a disease that interferes with her ability to walk, move her arms, see clearly, and learn. Cerebral palsy has no cure, although it is among the serious diseases scientists hope will one day be treated with therapies derived from stem cells. Such therapies are a long way from being available in the United States, where rigorous clinical trials have not yet deemed any such therapy safe or effective.

Yet in other countries with more relaxed rules, stem cell clinics are open and offering what they claim to be life-changing therapies to people like Kara Anderson. Desperate to help her, Kara's parents took her to one such clinic in China in December 2009, where they heard of doctors performing experimental stem cell injections that were not available in the United States.

After just two injections, Kara demonstrated amazing progress. Previously wheelchair bound, she was suddenly able to walk gingerly, with the aid of crutches, and walked for fifteen minutes on a treadmill, while holding a rail. She could also lift objects with her left hand and raise the hand over her head. Her eyesight also improved. Her parents were overjoyed. "We really weren't sure what to expect, but she got better and better every day," said Kara's father, Brian Anderson. "It was unbelievable."[1]

Stories like Kara's are attracting the attention of millions of hopeful sick people and launching them on journeys to India, Brazil, Russia, Panama, Thailand, the Caribbean, Ukraine, and elsewhere on the slim chance that stem cell treatments hold the key to a better, healthier life. In China alone more than two hundred stem cell clinics were in operation as of 2012. Yet this burgeoning "stem cell tourism" industry is deeply controversial, because the most renown stem cell research institutes in the world have not shown these therapies to be safe, effective, or reliable to treat the majority of diseases.

Doctors told the Andersons, for example, that cerebral palsy symptoms ebb and flow, and Kara's improvements could have been coincidental, a natural development and not a result of the treatments. Worse, some treatments could actually have dangerous side effects because they have been developed in the absence of clinical testing and rigorous federal oversight. The medical journal the *Lancet* reported in 2009, for example, that an Israeli boy developed spinal and brain tumors after undergoing stem cell treatments at a clinic in Moscow, Russia. "Unregulated therapy in the absence of any evidence that these cells are going to help patients is reckless," says Arnold Kreigstein, a neurologist who works with stem cells at the University of California, San Francisco. "The potential to do harm is enormous."[2]

Such procedures are also outrageously expensive. The treatments themselves cost tens of thousands of dollars, and families must also raise money to travel to another country and stay there for weeks at a time (Kara Anderson was in China for over a month). American stem cell researchers worry that people are being scammed out of their life's savings. Dr. Irving Weissman, a stem cell researcher at Stanford University, says he has heard multiple stories of people traveling to overseas clinics, only to see no improvement. "One [patient] paid $50,000 and the other paid $85,000 for treatments for untreatable genetic conditions," he said. "The clinics simply took their money, took their time, and of course didn't treat their conditions at all."[3]

Yet sick, suffering people are desperate to try anything for a shot at a healthy life. This is what sent one Canadian woman to China in 2007, where she sought stem cell therapy for multiple system atrophy, a degenerative disease similar to Parkinson's. Over four weeks of treatment, she received six stem cell injections, at a cost of $30,000. The clinic claimed to provide treatment for cerebral palsy, multiple sclerosis, muscular dystrophy, spinal cord injury, and other serious conditions, yet the woman's doctors in Canada expressed deep skepticism over the safety and efficacy of the treatment. Dominique McMahon, a postdoctoral fellow at the University of Toronto, says that in Canada, stem cell treatments have only proved effective for bone marrow transplants, skin grafting, and blood diseases, not for any of the conditions offered by clinics in China. McMahon is among many scientists who are therefore concerned about the legitimacy of these overseas clinics. "In some cases, it is not clear what is being injected," says McMahon. "There's no proof of safety and efficacy. The quality of facilities varies. The protocols are poorly documented and not available to the patients. Even in the best-case scenarios, the doctor doesn't know whether it's safe or efficacious because of a lack of data."[4]

The controversial stem cell tourism industry is just one of the many issues in the stem cell debate. The current volume, *Introducing Issues with Opposing Viewpoints: Stem Cell Research*, considers other arguments in the debate, such as whether stem cell research is moral, whether stem cell research can cure disease, and what role the government should play in funding and directing stem cell research. Students will examine these questions in the opposing viewpoint pairs and come to conclude for themselves whether stem cell research should be banned or whether its potential should be fully explored.

Notes

1. Quoted in Ariana Eunjung Cha, "With U.S. Stem Cell Treatments Limited, Patients Try Other Countries," *Washington Post*, June 6, 2010. www.washingtonpost.com/wp-dyn/content/article/2010/06/05/AR2010060502014.html.
2. Quoted in Cha, "With U.S. Stem Cell Treatments Limited, Patients Try Other Countries."
3. Quoted in Richard Knox, "Offshore Stem Cell Clinics Sell Hope, Not Science," National Public Radio," July 26, 2010. www.npr.org/templates/story/story.php?storyId=128696529.
4. Quoted in United Press International, "Stem Cell Tourism Can Be Pricey and Risky," February 11, 2012. www.upi.com/Health_News/2012/02/11/Stem-cell-tourism-can-be-pricey-and-risky/UPI-38901328943408/#ixzz1nz7DB1h2.

Chapter 1

Is Stem Cell Research Ethical?

Controversy over the ethics of stem cell research has raged over the last couple of decades in America and around the world.

Viewpoint

1

Embryonic Stem Cell Research Is Ethical

"The [anti-stem cell research decision] is an atrocity which will condemn whole generations to misery and denial of medical treatments in the future."

Paul Wallis

In the following viewpoint Paul Wallis argues that embryonic stem cell research is ethical. He is upset that certain groups have created obstacles for stem cell research based on their belief that it violates human life and dignity. Wallis argues that embryonic stem cell research does just the opposite: It could offer cures to millions of sick, disabled, and dying people. In his mind, it does this without compromising values, dignity, or experimenting on human beings. He contends that a blastocyst—the five- or six-day-old fertilized egg that consists of a small number of cells on which stem cell research is performed—is not yet a person. Wallis argues that people who seek to protect blastocysts over human beings have their priorities backward. He concludes that embryonic stem cell research could save and improve millions of lives and therefore is ethical.

Wallis is a journalist based in Sydney, Australia. His work is regularly featured in the *Digital Journal*.

In what can only be called one of the most insane decisions in legal history, the EU [European Union] Court of Justice [ECJ] has knocked back a patent for stem cells, stymieing the development of treatments which could cure millions of people of hideous medical conditions.

A Return to the Dark Ages

ABC Australia reports:

Stem cell technology is controversial because some cell lines are derived from embryos. The ECJ decision now endorses widespread protection of human embryos by blocking patents.

"A process which involves removal of a stem cell from a human embryo at the blastocyst stage, entailing the destruction of that embryo, cannot be patented," it said.

Blastocyst is the stage just before implantation in the womb, when the embryo consists of around 80 to 100 cells.

Typically, Christian groups are very pleased with this return to the Dark Ages. Just to prove how in touch with human misery they are, one group commented:

The European Centre for Law and Justice, a Strasbourg [France]-based Christian group, welcomed the decision which it said "protects life and human dignity" at all stages of development.

Stem Cell Research Protects Life and Dignity

It's so nice to know that people can have their lives protected and their dignity when living for decades in pain or with severe disabilities. It's also nice to know that these groups, which haven't raised a murmur in decades about the endless allegations of sexual abuse of children by the clergy, are in favour of people having more kids, and that every embryo should be protected. That's showing true respect for human life and dignity.

You'll also note that a blastocyst isn't actually an embryo—It's a collection of cells, and is "before implantation" in the womb, meaning the damn thing has no chance of becoming a human being unless "implanted". So we may assume that the ECJ isn't exactly paying attention to any relevant facts related to the actual physical status of the blastocyst, just basically saying "it might be an embryo". An external creation of a blastocyst, therefore, would also qualify as a potential baby, even though it has absolutely no chance of becoming one.

A stylized view of a blastocyst just before implantation in the womb, when the embryo consists of eighty to a hundred cells.

For the crimes of abortion, birth control, evolution, stem cell research....

SCIENCE

caglecartoons.com

A Few Should Not Dictate to the Rest

Again, a microscopic number of people are dictating policies related to human quality of life.

FAST FACT

In 2011 an annual Gallup poll found that 62 percent of Americans said embryonic stem cell research was moral, compared with just 52 percent who thought this in 2002.

Who elected these damn animals to have more say in medicine than doctors, the public, politicians or scientists?

Who said they had any right to deny possible cures to sick people?

There is no democracy, let alone sanity, in this process. On the basis of a small group of people's weird preferences, based on whatever series of "beliefs of convenience" they may have, science and medicine can be derailed. It's like the old days hundreds of years ago when the Church banned anatomical studies. The Church effectively put back medicine for centuries.

It's doing it again. Again, perhaps decades from now, perhaps centuries, stem cell technology, like surgery and other modern medical practices, will eventually be common practice.

One Faith Should Not Hold Everyone Back

There's another issue here, which may interest some Americans—If you have freedom of worship, and the actions of a court effectively imposes the values of someone else's beliefs on you, your rights are being infringed, particularly if you suffer as a result.

If you're a Buddhist, Sikh, Anglican, pagan or any other religion, why should your rights to medical treatment be affected by a court decision which has absolutely no basis but the values of another religion?

Embryonic Stem Cell Research Enjoys Wide Support

A 2010 poll found the majority of Americans of all political persuasions and major religious backgrounds approve of research on stem cells derived from human embryos.

Question: "Stem cells come from embryos, left over from in vitro fertilization, which are not used and normally destroyed. Many medical researchers want to use them to develop treatments or to prevent diseases such as diabetes, Alzheimer's or Parkinson's disease. Do you think this research should be allowed or not be allowed?"

	All Adults	Party			Religion			
		Republican	Democrat	Independent	Catholic	Protestant	Other Christian/ Other Religion	Born-Again Christian
Should be allowed	72%	58%	82%	73%	69%	74%	66%	58%
Should not be allowed	12%	24%	4%	10%	16%	11%	15%	22%
Not sure	17%	18%	13%	18%	16%	14%	19%	20%

Percentages may not add up exactly to 100% due to rounding.

Taken from: Harris Interactive, 2010.

There's no medical or scientific basis to assume a blastocyst is anything more than a collection of cells, for practical purposes.

There's no legal precedent or even a working legal rationale for blocking intellectual property related to any *other* form of medical research.

It's only religion which condemns stem cell research.

Support Stem Cell Research

The ECJ decision is an atrocity which will condemn whole generations to misery and denial of medical treatments in the future. This decision is the enabling act for a future lifelong medical Auschwitz[1] affecting millions of people.

It's too much to hope that that dismal collection of failed money launderers running Europe will have either the intellect or the knowledge to reverse the decision or pass laws enabling the research to proceed without the interference of superstition and ignoramuses.

The research will probably gravitate to China, and other countries where 2000 year old drivel isn't a matter of public policy.

I hope the ECJ is happy.

> **EVALUATING THE AUTHOR'S ARGUMENTS:**
>
> In making his argument, Paul Wallis claims that people who oppose embryonic stem cell research violate other people's rights. What does he mean by this? Flesh out his position in three to four sentences. Then, state whether or not you agree, and why.

1. Auschwitz was a Nazi concentration camp where millions of people were killed during the Holocaust.

Embryonic Stem Cell Research Is Unethical

> *"The problem with embryonic stem cell research is that the goals are so desirable that they override our usual moral impulses."*

Steve Chapman

In the following viewpoint Steve Chapman argues that embryonic stem cell research is unethical because it requires the destruction of a five-day-old embryo, known as a blastocyst. In Chapman's view, destroying a blastocyst is similar to murder: If implanted into a woman's womb, it would develop into a fetus, and then a baby. Chapman says supporters of embryonic stem cell research blind themselves to this fact. They are so tempted by the cures promised by this research, he contends, that they become willing to do inhumane, unethical things to reach this end. He concludes that embryonic stem cell research carries too high a price to be considered ethical or practical.

Chapman is a syndicated columnist for the *Chicago Tribune*.

AS YOU READ, CONSIDER THE FOLLOWING QUESTIONS:
1. What does Chapman say Congress decreed about federal funding of stem cell research in 1996?
2. What, in the author's view, is different about destroying a five-
   day-old embryo than a five-week-old or five-month-old one?
3. How does former president George W. Bush's stem cell research
   policy compare with President Barack Obama's policy, as
   described by Chapman?

When he announced his policy expanding federal funding of embryonic stem cell research, President Barack Obama was not timid about proclaiming its benefits. It would, he announced, hasten "a day when words like 'terminal' and 'incurable' are finally retired from our vocabulary."

You thought Obama wanted to establish death panels? Actually, he seems to think he can confer immortality.

An Overly Confident Claim

That announcement, made in March of last year [2009] dismantled the limits imposed by the [George W.] Bush administration. The change, in Obama's view, was a triumph over ignorance and ideology.

His executive order was, the president claimed, "about protecting free and open inquiry" and letting scientists "do their jobs, free from manipulation and coercion, and listening to what they tell us, even when it's inconvenient." When science wins, he led us to believe, we all win.

Conspicuously absent from those declarations were facts that Obama would prefer to omit because they are—well, inconvenient. But those facts did not elude U.S. District Judge Royce Lamberth, who on Monday [August 23, 2010] said the revised policy violates federal law.[1]

The Law Forbids Killing Embryos

What facts? A restriction approved by Congress in 1996, and repeat-edly renewed, says federal money may not be used for "research in

---

1. Lamberth's ruling was put on hold in September 2010 and then dropped in July 2011, once again permit-ting federal funding for embryonic stem cell research.

which a human embryo or embryos are destroyed." But the point of Obama's new policy was to pay for experiments using stem cells harvested from embryos that are killed in the process.

The administration evaded the ban by stipulating that Washington could fund such research as long as it didn't fund the part where the fetus is terminated. Judge Lamberth was not buying.

Embryonic stem cell research, he noted, requires the destruction of embryos. The federal prohibition, he said, "encompasses *all* 'research in which' an embryo is destroyed, not just the 'piece of research' in

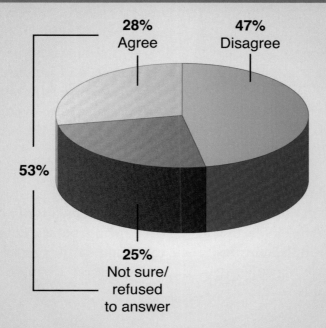

Americans Are Troubled by the Morality of Stem Cell Research

Although more Americans support embryonic stem cell research than oppose it, the majority—53 percent—think it is either wrong to put science ahead of life, or are unsure about it.

"We should not put the interests of medical science ahead of the preservation of human life, which includes human embryos."

28% Agree

47% Disagree

53%

25% Not sure/ refused to answer

Taken from: Harris Interactive, October 7, 2010.

which the embryo is destroyed." So any funding of experiments using such stem cells is forbidden.

Obama imagines that this research may make the word "terminal" obsolete—except, of course, when applied to the embryos that perish when their stem cells are taken for scientific inquiry.

What's Wrong with Destroying Embryos?

President George W. Bush's policy allowed research only on stem cell lines that had already been established. The idea was to facilitate studies without creating incentives to destroy additional embryos.

Obama, by contrast, took the view that the destruction of additional embryos (those "left over" at fertility clinics) is essential to the march of science.

> ## FAST FACT
>
> A 2010 CNN poll found that just 40 percent of Republicans believe the federal government should fund research that involves stem cells obtained from human embryos; 58 percent feel the government should not be involved in this kind of research.

What's wrong with destroying a 5-day-old embryo that would be discarded anyway? Nothing, unless you think there is something wrong with killing a human embryo ostensibly for some greater good.

If there is nothing wrong with that, though, it's hard to see what's wrong with destroying an embryo that is 5 weeks old or 5 months old, if its tissue could be used to help people who are seriously ill. In that case, why limit research to leftover embryos? It would make more sense to let scientists create embryos and let them gestate for months, for the sole purpose of destroying them for their stem cells.

The Ends Must Not Blind Us to the Means

Americans might bridle at that prospect, but proponents of expanded embryonic stem cell research have spared them from the contemplation of such unpleasantness. Their campaign focuses on ends, not means—alleviating suffering, conquering disease, letting the blind see and the lame walk.

On March 9, 2009, President Barack Obama signed a bill that lifted restrictions on federal funding for embryonic stem cell research.

Such advances are only speculative at this point. But their allure is such as to discourage us from looking too closely at the methods needed to bring them about. It's easier to think in terms of excising tissue from blastocysts than in terms of killing human embryos. In reality, they are the same thing.

The problem with embryonic stem cell research is that the goals are so desirable that they override our usual moral impulses. Yuval Levin, a fellow at the Ethics and Public Policy Center in Washington, wrote in 2006 in *The New Atlantis*, "It is very hard for us to describe something higher than health, or more important than the relief of suffering, so when relief comes at a cost, even the cost of cherished principles or self-evident truths, we all too often pay up."

The court decision against Obama's policy on stem cell research is a rare exception, which may induce us to reconsider the wisdom of what we have sanctioned. "Our problem is not that we are lacking in ethical principles," says Levin, "but rather that we are forgetful of them."

EVALUATING THE AUTHORS' ARGUMENTS:

Steve Chapman and Paul Wallis (the author of the previous viewpoint) disagree on whether it is moral to destroy a five-day-old embryo (called a blastocyst). Chapman regards it as the killing of a human; Wallis regards it as destroying prehuman cells that will die anyway. After reading both viewpoints, with which author do you agree, and why?

Stem Cell Research Can Lead to Cloning and Other Scientific Atrocities

"Humanzees ... may be fanciful creations. The mass production of human-animal embryos may not."

Paige C. Cunnningham

In the following viewpoint Paige C. Cunningham warns that stem cell research could lead to scientific atrocities, such as the development of human-animal hybrid creatures. She discusses how, already, some scientists have created such hybrids in order to extract embryonic stem cells from them. She envisions a day in which such creatures will be produced en masse in order to supply tissues, organs, and other medical materials to needy patients. According to Cunningham, the morality of such a process is unclear, as is whether, if such creatures are part human, they should be accorded human rights. She warns that the field of stem cell research is fraught with many critical ethical questions that have no easy answers.

Paige C. Cunningham, "Ligers, Tigons, and Splice: Human-Animal Hybrids," *The Center for Bioethics & Human Dignity,* May 20, 2011. Copyright © 2011 by The Center for Bioethics & Human Dignity, Trinity International University. All rights reserved. Reproduced by permission.

Cunningham is the executive director of the Center for Bioethics and Human Dignity, an institute that uses a Judeo-Christian framework to interpret bioethical issues.

AS YOU READ, CONSIDER THE FOLLOWING QUESTIONS:
1. What is a cybrid, as described by the author?
2. From what does Cunningham say Chinese scientists claim embryonic stem cells could be harvested?
3. What does the word *zoonotic* mean as used by the author?

In the popular understanding, [the term] "hybrids" includes three biotechnologies: chimeras, hybrids, and cybrids. Chimeras are entities created by mixing cells of different animals, usually two different species; each cell retains its original genetic identity. Think of a graft, such as replacing an aging human heart valve with one grown in a pig. Other chimeras are created at a much earlier stage by mixing two embryos, changing the appearance of the new organism. While the centaur is a mythological version, unusual animal hybrids exist, for example, the liger (a combination of a male lion and female tiger), the tigon (offspring of a male tiger and female lion), and the beefalo, a bison/cattle breed designed for beef production.

Splice, a 2010 summer movie release, tells the dark tale of Dren, a half-human, half-animal lab-created chimera that unpredictably grows and terrorizes people. Actual human chimeras may not raise the same fears. Their new heart valve does not acquire human DNA. Nor does it change their fundamental humanness.

Creating Hybrids to Harvest Stem Cells

True hybrids are created by integrating some genetic material from one species into an animal of a different species, perhaps by fertilizing the egg of the former with sperm from the latter. Human "cybrids" are hybrids created by a cloning process: human DNA is inserted into a non-human egg that has been enucleated (the animal nucleus has been removed), usually from a cow or rabbit. Cybrids contain more than 99% human DNA; the rabbit or cow mitochondrial DNA in the cytoplasm surrounding the nucleus remains. The United Kingdom, one of few places to permit cybrid research, requires the cybrid embryo to be destroyed after fourteen days. Chinese scientists apparently created a human-animal [HA] hybrid by inserting human DNA into rabbit eggs for the purpose of extracting the embryonic stem cells.

HA hybrids are produced for a variety of purposes: to observe how transplanted cells differentiate in the host (*What kinds of cells do they become?*), to test human cells (*Are these early cells pluripotent?*), to find out what cells will do (*Will these become cancerous?*), to reveal how these cells are affected by different control systems, to test new drugs for medical treatment, and to grow replacement tissues or organs for xenotransplantation [transplanting tissues or organs from one species into another]. As the Chinese have claimed, embryonic stem cells might be harvested from cybrid embryos. Their research, which has not been proven elsewhere, would produce human embryos in bulk, to create made-to-order tissues for patients.

Opponents of stem cell research warn it will lead to the creation of freakish, unnatural hybrids, such as this sheep/goat chimera (which contains a mixture of genetically different tissues from a sheep and a goat).

Some Benefits, but Also Serious Risks

HA hybrids might be used to study the causes and development of diseases such as cystic fibrosis, Parkinson's, AIDS and heart disease, pointing toward new therapies. Genetically engineered mice hybrids with human DNA inserted can generate antibodies to treat cancer that will not be rejected by the human recipient's body. Researchers may also develop HA hybrids to test new drugs.

Despite their significant research potential, HA hybrids carry some risks. The lessons of history warn of the risk of zoonotic infection. That is, diseases which have been confined to the animal kingdom may cross over to humans. We have witnessed the worldwide calamities triggered by the introduction of HIV, avian virus, and H1N1 influenza (swine flu). A single genetic or protein fragment might be sufficient for crossing the species boundary, causing diseases such as cancer, leukemia, and mad cow disease.

> **FAST FACT**
>
> As of 2012, researchers from a variety of countries had cloned more than twenty-three kinds of animals, including: camel, carp, cat, cattle, deer, dog, ferret, frog, fruit flies, goat, horse, mice, mule, pig, rabbit, rat, sheep, water buffalo, and wolf.

Additional risks include the creation of human diseases and the reality that no one knows how the HA hybrids will develop. When animal viruses cross the species barrier, new strains can emerge which may be carried only by human hosts. Furthermore, while many animal hybrids are sterile, closely related species, such as a mule and a donkey, have been known to reproduce. The "what if" allure of inseminating a primate, such as a chimpanzee, with human sperm may be irresistible. The sensationalized attempt of an early 20th century Soviet scientist to create "humanzees" dramatically illustrates this potential.

Ethical Concerns Abound

Ethical inquiry often begins with questions about consequences. As HA experiments proceed, what would be the moral status of these new creatures? Are they protected by animal welfare regulations, or do they

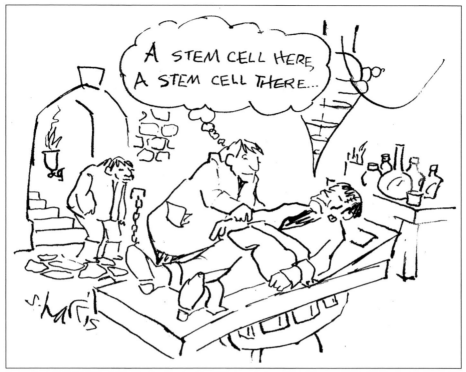

"A stem cell here, a stem cell there . . ." cartoon by Harris, S., www.CartoonStock.com, Copyright © Harris, S. Reproduction rights obtainable from www.CartoonStock.com.

deserve human subject research protection? Are there limitations on how much human DNA can be inserted into an animal? How are the risks of zoonotic infection controlled? Would this open the door to using primates to grow donor specific replacement organs, as did the mad scientists in Robin Cook's [novel] *Chromosome*? . . .

It is important to note that not all HA hybrid research may violate species boundaries. Inserting a small fragment of human DNA into a mouse to develop a cancer-fighting drug, for example, might not implicate human dignity. Growing a human-tolerant pig valve for a heart patient is therapeutic, not threatening.

These potentially life-saving examples do not resolve the many ethical considerations that remain. What about concerns for animal welfare? The host animal and its offspring may suffer terribly. Could "human dignity" apply to HA hybrids? Are they human, or actually something else? In addition to neurons, are there other types of cells that raise specific concerns, such as gametes [reproductive cells], or organs, such as the uterus? Does it matter at what stage of biological development the species mixing occurs? It could be at fertilization, at the embryonic stage, or somewhat later. How is this relevant?

Science Fiction Is Here and Real

Humanzees or Dren from *Splice* may be fanciful creations. The mass production of human-animal embryos may not. Somewhere in between we may find the highest and best purposes of research, those therapeutic goals that do not violate ethical standards. We still lack a Christian consensus on all aspects of the HA hybrid question, but we must persevere and continue the difficult work of thinking through ethical issues, principles, and their application. A premature conclusion may initially satisfy, but ultimately prove to be a barrier to both encouraging ethical research and respecting human dignity in all its stages, ages, and variations.

EVALUATING THE AUTHORS' ARGUMENTS:

Both Paige C. Cunningham and Arthur Caplan (author of the following viewpoint) are bioethicists that work for bioethical institutes, yet they take different positions on whether stem cell research will lead to cloning, human-animal hybrids, or other scientific atrocities. Cunningham sees a great probability of this; Caplan thinks it is unlikely. After reading both authors' perspectives, what do you think? Will pursuing stem cell research send science down a dangerous path? Explain your reasoning.

Stem Cell Research Will Not Likely Lead to Cloning or Other Scientific Atrocities

Arthur Caplan

"No frothing murderous human clones are ever coming to get you. [These] doomed, misprogrammed embryo-like eggs . . . are not people when created and cannot become people later."

In the following viewpoint Arthur Caplan argues that stem cell research will not lead to human cloning or other scientific atrocities. He says that scientists have been unable to clone a human, and there is little indication they will become able, or even be interested in doing so. According to Caplan, the kind of cloning involved in stem cell research involves creating an embryo that has three, rather than two, sets of genes. This means it is fundamentally not human and cannot survive beyond a few days, after valuable stem cells are extracted from it. But the embryo itself is not a person nor is it capable of becoming one. In Caplan's opinion, it is wrong to scare people away from stem cell research by pitching them mad scientist horror stories. He concludes stem cell research is ethical and will not result in human cloning.

Caplan is director of the Center for Bioethics at the University of Pennsylvania.

AS YOU READ, CONSIDER THE FOLLOWING QUESTIONS:
1. What group does Caplan say successfully cloned a human embryo in October 2011?
2. What does the phrase "fix-it kit" mean as used by the author?
3. What, according to Caplan, ought cloning be about?

There is nothing like an advance in human cloning to grab everyone's attention. So [the October 5, 2011,] news that scientists at the New York Stem Cell Foundation have successfully cloned a human embryo and produced apparently viable stem cells has the whole world watching.

Should we be concerned that the clones are coming to your town—and soon? Hardly. Is the new research of keen interest if you have a damaged spinal column, Parkinson's disease, juvenile diabetes or a seriously damaged heart? Absolutely. The technique involved should quiet the opponents of human embryonic stem cell research because, while cloning is involved, the creation of viable human embryos is not.

FAST FACT

As of 2012, all claims of human cloning have been proven false. In 2002 Dr. Brigitte Boisselier, a chemistry professor and CEO of a company called Clonaid, claimed her religious cult, the Raelians, had successfully cloned a human girl, though no proof was ever offered. In 2005 South Korean scientist Hwang Woo-suk was discovered to have lied about having cloned human embryos for stem cell research.

It Is Not Possible to Clone Humans

Scientists have been trying to clone human embryos from the cells of the human body ever since Dolly the [cloned] sheep was announced in 1997. The cloning efforts are not to make people, but to find a way to create personalized health repair kits. If you could make an embryo using

DNA extracted from one of the cells in your skin, liver or muscle, then stem cells could be made that are biologically identical to your other cells. This would allow doctors potentially to fix a wide variety of diseases in your body without having the repair cells attacked as foreign invaders.

The problem with this idea—a fix-it kit for each of us from the DNA of our own cells—is that cloning has not worked. At all.

Despite a lot of claims by con artists, frauds and nuts, no one in over 15 years has been able to clone a human embryo, much less make a cloned human being. Even though a slew of magazine and Internet articles have long hinted that human cloning is just around the corner, the corner has proven to be more like a chain of mountains.

The author says fears that stem cell research will lead to human cloning are misplaced and not based on facts.

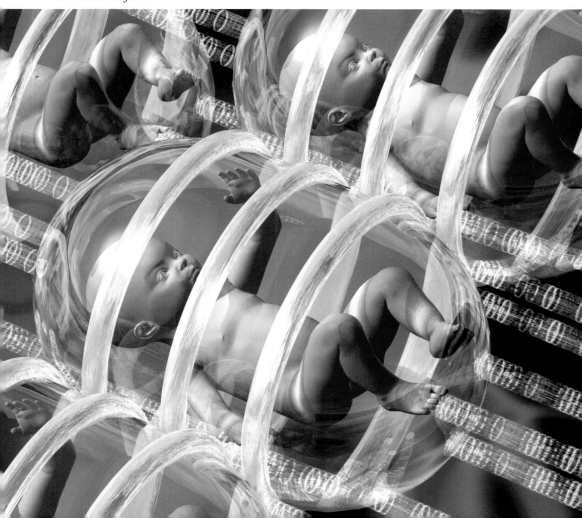

Most People Trust Scientists

A 2010 Harris Poll found the majority of Americans trust scientists to perform appropriate and ethical stem cell research that will be used to treat disease.

"If most scientists believe that stem cell research will greatly increase our ability to prevent or treat serious diseases we should trust them and let them do it."

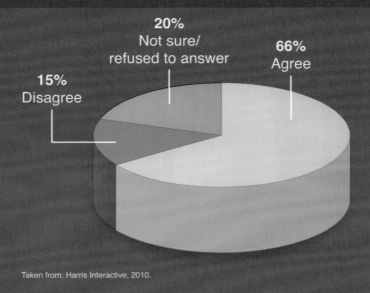

20%
Not sure/ refused to answer

66%
Agree

15%
Disagree

Taken from: Harris Interactive, 2010.

"No Frothing Murderous Human Clones"

The New York research shows there is a way to get cloning to work—sort of. The scientists involved found that if they moved DNA from an adult cell and stuck it into a donated human egg without removing the egg's DNA, then an embryo would start to grow. In traditional cloning, the DNA is pulled out of the egg and replaced by the DNA transferred from skin, liver or other body cell. While useful for making sheep and horses and goats—for people, not so much. The new technique creates a genetic overflow in the cloned egg, but it was partly successful.

The good news is, the newly cloned eggs in this research have three sets of genes and die after a couple of days. That means no frothing murderous human clones are ever coming to get you. And making doomed, misprogrammed embryo-like eggs should put an end to the fear-mongering used to attack funding for research on cloning to create embryonic stem cells. They are not people when created and cannot become people later.

Even better news: You can get stem cells out of the gene-heavy cloned eggs that do seem to work like embryonic stem cells. That means possible repair kit cells could be made from your own cells someday and used to treat your particular diseases.

These Embryos Are Not Really People

It is still exceedingly early to see if this approach to cloning really can be used to make useful 'embryonic' stem cells. But, it is not too early to understand that the work using this type of cloning ought to be funded and supported. The human 'embryos' made by this form of gene transfer are not people.

No one wants to try and turn them into people and even if they did they could not do so. They are human embryos only if you stretch the term embryo to its very limit.

So there is a potential way to make embryonic stem cells using cloning, but nothing ethically to worry about. This is cloning as it ought to be—making cells, not people.

EVALUATING THE AUTHOR'S ARGUMENTS:

In this viewpoint, Arthur Caplan uses facts, examples, and reasoning to make his argument that stem cell research will not result in human cloning. He does not, however, use any quotations to support his point. If you were to rewrite this article and insert quotations, from what authorities might you quote? Where would you place quotations, and why?

Chapter 2

Can Stem Cell Research Cure Disease?

A researcher uses a cell-sorting machine to isolate stem cells from adult bone marrow. Deciding what types of stem cells to use for research is at the center of the debate.

Embryonic Stem Cell Research Will Cure Many Diseases

Michael J. Fox

"As a person with Parkinson's it's hugely frustrating to think that one decision can actively hold back research that holds promise to transform lives."

In the following viewpoint actor Michael J. Fox argues that embryonic stem cell research can yield cures for some of life's most devastating diseases—if only scientists would be allowed to pursue their work. He contends that embryonic stem cells offer the most promise for curing terrible diseases like Parkinson's, from which he suffers. He is angry that politics and misinformation cause people to oppose this research. When they do, he says, they stand directly in his way of experiencing a better, healthier life. Fox concludes that he and others deserve to benefit from the cures that will be offered by unobstructed embryonic stem cell research.

Fox first became famous in the 1980s for starring in the TV series *Family Ties* and such movies as *Back to the Future* and *Teenwolf*. He was diagnosed with Parkinson's in 1991 and has since become an outspoken advocate for stem cell research.

AS YOU READ, CONSIDER THE FOLLOWING QUESTIONS:
1. What finding did scientists make about the spinal fluid of Alzheimer's patients, according to Fox?
2. What is a biomarker, as defined by the author?
3. What percentage of Americans does Fox report support more funding for stem cell research?

Biomedical research is complicated. For patients, the pace of progress can be frustratingly slow. Two announcements last month [August 2010]—one about biomarkers, the other about stem cell research—left many of us feeling that for every promising discovery, there are even greater setbacks.

Breakthroughs and Setbacks

We started August with good news about the discovery of an Alzheimer's biological marker in spinal fluid that will allow earlier diagnosis of patients who are experiencing some memory loss. It may not sound sexy. But for Alzheimer's patients and their loved ones, the significance of this finding is hard to overstate.

Biomarkers, which are substances or characteristics in our bodies that are associated with the risk or presence of disease, are critical tools in the quest for therapies that can slow or stop the progression of neurodegenerative diseases. Until now, Alzheimer's researchers, like those in the Parkinson's field have not had the benefit of a biomarker to guide their discovery.

> **FAST FACT**
>
> In 2011 researchers at the Memorial Sloan-Kettering Cancer Centre in New York reported they grew, from embryonic stem cells, the brain cells that die off when a person suffers from Parkinson's disease.

This major breakthrough was the result of an unprecedented data sharing and collaboration. A consortium of scientists and executives across academia, government, industry, and the nonprofit world pooled their collective interests into one larger, collaborative platform, the Alzheimer's Disease Neuroimaging Initiative (ADNI). In just six years—a relatively short time in biomedical research—they announced success.

A Critical Obstacle to Progress

But with this one step forward came two steps backward two weeks ago when a U.S. judge granted a preliminary injunction to halt federal funding for embryonic stem cell research.

This ruling, which is even more restrictive than President [George W.] Bush's stem cell research policies, goes against the beliefs of the majority of Americans (in an August 2010 poll conducted by Research America, 70 percent of respondents said they favor expanded funding for stem cell research) and wastes more precious time for the millions of people suffering from chronic diseases.

Since being diagnosed with Parkinson's disease, actor Michael J. Fox (at podium) has been an outspoken advocate of stem cell research. Here he is joined by members of the US House and Senate in urging passage of legislation furthering stem cell research.

Why Embryonic Stem Cells Are Special

Embryonic stem cells are *undifferentiated*, which means they have the potential to turn into any other kind of cell. Although non-embryonic adult stem cells and induced pluripotent stem (iPS) cells have also shown promise, researchers say they are more limited, and thus potentially less powerful and versatile, than embryonic stem cells.

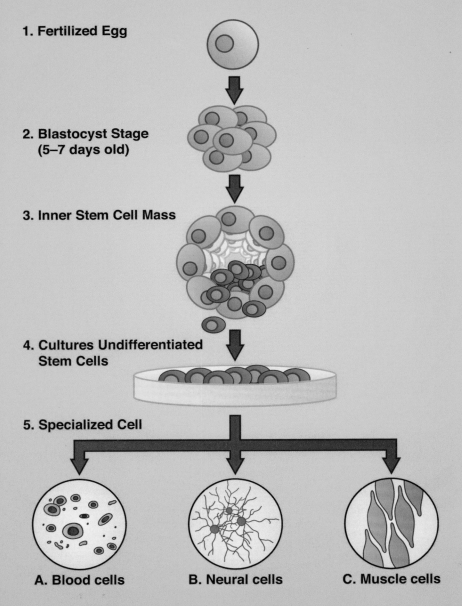

1. Fertilized Egg

2. Blastocyst Stage (5–7 days old)

3. Inner Stem Cell Mass

4. Cultures Undifferentiated Stem Cells

5. Specialized Cell

A. Blood cells

B. Neural cells

C. Muscle cells

Taken from: http://stemcells-research.net.

Let Scientists Find Cures for People Like Me

As a person with Parkinson's, it's hugely frustrating to think that one decision can actively hold back research that holds promise to transform lives. Patients with neurodegenerative diseases dream of the day when disease-modifying treatments are found, instead of therapies that simply mask symptoms. Disease-modifying therapies create the possibility of newly diagnosed patients never having to experience full-blown disease.

The Michael J. Fox Foundation has long championed the scientific freedom to pursue all promising paths to finding these treatments. Biomarker discovery and stem cell science are among the innovative areas of biomedical research that hold potential to speed progress.

So while our foundation gears up to launch its most ambitious biomarker discovery project to date, the Parkinson's Progression Markers Initiative, with ADNI as a precedent, we'll also be standing with Parkinson's patients, their loved ones and the majority of Americans who want us to move beyond political agendas and advance the promise of stem cell research.

> **EVALUATING THE AUTHOR'S ARGUMENTS:**
>
> Michael J. Fox personalizes this issue by explaining that he suffers from a disease that could be cured by embryonic stem cell research. He says people who oppose stem cell research stand in his way of having a better life. What do you think of this tactic? Does it make you want to agree with Fox, to support research that could improve his life? Or does his personal experience not factor into your opinion of stem cell research? Explain your reasoning.

The Curative Power of Embryonic Stem Cells Has Been Exaggerated

Mary Carmichael

"But critics, including the American Academy of Pediatrics, accuse private cord-blood banks like CBR of making exaggerated medical promises and exploiting vulnerable new parents."

In the following viewpoint Mary Carmichael argues that media often exaggerate the curative nature of embryonic stem cells. She claims that private cord banks, which harvest stem cells from the umbilical cord, exploit vulnerable new parents and cord cell uses are limited at best. Although these cells have been shown to improve certain diseases in some cases, the claim of a miraculous cure has been exaggerated and the cord contains only enough stem cells to treat a small child.

Carmichael is general editor of *Newsweek* magazine.

AS YOU READ, CONSIDER THE FOLLOWING QUESTIONS:
1. Who is Joanne Kurtzberg?
2. How many samples are contained in the world's largest private cord blood bank, as stated in the article?
3. According to the author, has there been a radical rise in the uses for cord blood cells?

Dallas Hextell was just a baby when his parents bought him a walker—not because he was late reaching a milestone, but because they worried he might never toddle on his own. At 9 months he had been diagnosed with cerebral palsy, a form of brain injury caused by oxygen deprivation in utero or at birth. A neurologist had told Derak and Cynthia Hextell there was no cure, that it was best to wait and see if their son improved. But Cynthia, after months of research, enrolled Dallas in a highly experimental trial at Duke University, where a pediatric-transplant surgeon infused him with a sample of his own stem cells harvested from his umbilical-cord blood. A few days later, Derak and Cynthia went home with their son, who was 18 months old and still not crawling, much less walking or talking. They "stared at him" for a week, says Cynthia. "One day he just started saying, 'Mama, mama, mama.' And I started crying." The Hextells ended up donating the walker to another child. By 2, Dallas was not only walking unaided, he was chasing the family dogs.

If the Hextells' names sound familiar to some readers, it is because, in the wake of their son's remarkable recovery, they have become minor celebrities. Their story has appeared on the "Today" show and in advertisements in almost every pregnancy magazine in the country. The ads are not for the trial at Duke, which remains a small, academic endeavor. They are for a company called Cord Blood Registry [CBR], which charges parents $2,000-plus to freeze and store samples of their children's umbilical-cord blood, a fluid rich in stem cells. Cynthia Hextell paid the company to freeze Dallas's cord blood at his birth. That sample was the source of the stem cells used in the Duke trial—and as the ads remind parents, it was available only because the Hextells had paid for it to be.

The Hextells' story has become the centerpiece of CBR's marketing efforts. Recently the company invited about 30 obstetricians and midwives to the Westin La Paloma resort in Tucson, Ariz., for a weekend of sun, golf and medical briefings, including dinner in a ballroom with the Hextells as guest speakers. Since these doctors had collected cord blood for CBR clients in the past, the company hoped to turn them into evangelists. The next day, the group went for a tour of CBR's glittering 60,000-square-foot lab. The agenda also included more time at the La Paloma, home to a Jack Nicklaus golf course, a spa, five restaurants and a swim-up bar. CBR can easily afford to put on this kind of show. Ten years ago it was a fledgling business with 10,000 clients. Today it is the country's largest private cord-blood bank, with 250,000 samples in storage, 300 employees and $100 million in annual revenue.

Medicine and Money

In medicine, money often comes with controversy—and right now, CBR has plenty of both. The company says it is providing precious biological insurance, that to freeze a child's cord-blood stem cells is to provide him a medical option for the future, perhaps a lifesaving treatment for childhood cancer or brain injuries. But critics, including the American Academy of Pediatrics, accuse private cord-blood banks like CBR of making exaggerated medical promises and exploiting vulnerable new parents. Cord blood's uses are limited at best, they say. The blood does not provide enough cells to cure an adult of a disease or injury; it is not appropriate for treating genetic conditions; and thus far there have been few trials to determine how effectively the cells can repair damaged tissue. Even Joanne Kurtzberg, the Duke transplant specialist who treated Dallas Hextell, is skeptical. She says it's difficult to know if his improvement is related to the cells or would have occurred without them—he probably would have gotten better on his own; some cerebral-palsy patients do—and she points out that her trial is small and yet to be analyzed and published. But CBR has a response for this. It says more uses for cord-blood stem cells will surely be discovered in the future. It also knows the power of a good story. David Zitlow, the company's senior vice president of public affairs, says doctors "haven't made a big enough deal about anecdotes" like the Hextells'.

Embryonic Stem Cells Versus Induced Pluripotent Stem Cells

Embryonic stem cells are harvested from five-day-old embryos. Induced pluripotent stem (iPS) cells are made by reprogramming adult skin cells. Thus, their use is less controversial since they do not require the use or destruction of any embryos.

Embryonic Stem Cells
Therapeutic Cloning

Egg Cell Body Cell

Nucleus removed   Nucleus removed

Nucleus from the body cells inserted into egg cell

Cloned cell induced to form an embryo

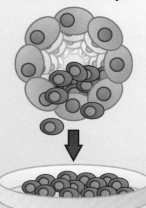

Stem cells harvested from embryo cells

Induced Pluripotent Stem Cells
Nuclear Reprogramming

Skin Cells

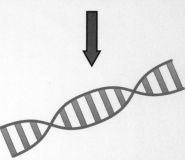

Genes inserted to induce reprogramming

Reprogrammed cells resemble embryonic stem cells

So what are other parents, faced with the choice of banking their children's cord blood or brushing off the idea as a luxury—the medical equivalent of an $800 stroller—supposed to make of Dallas Hextell's case? Is it a breakthrough, a harbinger? Or is it ultimately just an anecdote, a moving tale with a happy outcome that may or may not have anything to do with cord blood and stem cells?

Doctors have been wondering if cord blood is something of a miracle cure for the past 15 years. The blood—which is usually thrown away in delivery rooms—contains a distinct type of stem cell that may act as a biochemical foreman, helping to build healthy tissues and repair damaged ones. In the early 1990s—before embryonic stem cells took over the spotlight—researchers began to explore whether cord-blood cells might be of practical medical use. At Duke, Kurtzberg performed a few cord-blood transplants on patients with leukemia and rare types of bone-marrow failure, sending them into remission. Meanwhile, the National Institutes of Health started funding public banks of frozen, donated cord-blood samples, modeled on adult blood banks. A cord-blood stem-cell transplant at that point was a long shot, an experiment to see if stem cells could either become new tissue or trick the body into fixing itself. But the idea behind the public banks was to make the option available to all families who might want to try it as a last resort. . . .

A number of trends have likely contributed to CBR's growth, including the enormous boom in the baby-products market and the hype around stem cells in general. But one thing that has not been a factor is a rapid rise in medical uses for cord blood—because there hasn't been one yet. Just as it was in the '90s, a cord-blood stem-cell transplant is still an experimental procedure. This hasn't deterred CBR from publicizing the results of a few positive studies, including a small, preliminary trial in kids with type 1 diabetes from last year.

Cord-Blood Treatment a Miracle?

In Dallas Hextell, CBR has another case to promote. In ads, the Hextells call the cord-blood treatment "a miracle." But nobody really knows what has happened in Dallas's brain. The story sounds less clear-cut coming from Kurtzberg, the doctor who performed the transfusion and who examined Dallas again in November. "He has made progress, there's no question," she says. "But he still has a global developmental delay of about a year. He looks like where we would have expected him to be without cells." When she saw him at his follow-up visit, she adds, "I thought, wow, he doesn't look as good as I was expecting based on what's been in the press." (The Hextells find Kurtzberg's assessment frustrating and note that Dallas's therapists at home—who knew him before the transfusion—are impressed and surprised at his improvement.) Kurtzberg also has not completed the follow-up and analysis of the study or published the results from 50 other kids with cerebral palsy who have enrolled in her trial thus far.

Kurtzberg, it turns out, is not a big booster for private cord-blood banks; although she uses samples from CBR, she does not receive funding from the company, and also uses cells from public banks and other companies. In fact, she's one of the authors of a statement the American Academy of Pediatrics [AAP] put out last year

[in 2007] discouraging parents from using private banks on the grounds that the science isn't solid enough yet to justify a multi-thousand-dollar gamble. (The AAP does support public, nonprofit banks, which patients can use for free.) The American College of Obstetricians and Gynecologists released its own statement in February, noting that "there is no reliable estimate of a child's likelihood of actually using his or her own saved cord blood later." Then it made a guess anyway: 1 in 2,700, which Kurtzberg calls "generous."

Why is this number so small? There are reasons to think cord-blood treatment will never be a widespread medical procedure. The blood contains only enough stem cells to treat a small child; unlike embryonic stem cells, cord-blood cells cannot be multiplied into self-rejuvenating "lines" in a petri dish. The cells are limited in other ways, too. There's little point in treating a genetic condition with a patient's own cord-blood cells, which have the same DNA and thus the same deleterious mutations. Scientists could someday overcome

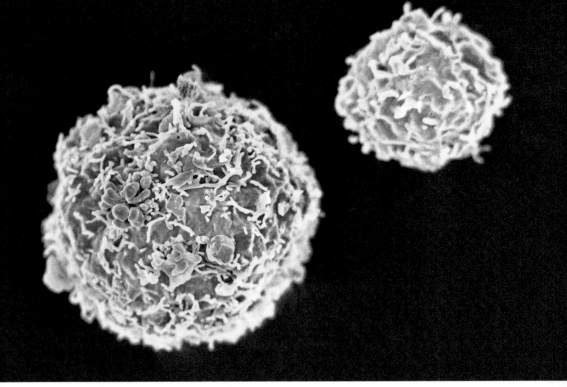

Pluripotent adult stem cells do not require the destruction of embryos, and their genes can be reprogrammed.

these hurdles; they could develop new ways of cultivating and genetically tweaking cord-blood cells in the lab. But by then, the same scientists will probably know much more about all stem cells, especially once restrictions on embryonic research are lifted—and there may be better ways of getting safe, usable cells from other sources, ways that won't require a lot of technological wizardry.

Widespread Trials Needed

These difficulties don't deter everyone, of course. The pediatrician Robert Sears, a talk-show regular and the coauthor of popular parenting books, supports private cord-blood banking; he froze his own kids' samples with CBR. It's also possible that 1 in 2,700 is too conservative. CBR's executives toss around much more dramatic odds. Harris, the scientific director, puts them at a breathtaking 1 in 3. His calculations, unlike the professional groups', include injuries to the brain. There is, he notes, "no genetic predisposition to falling out of a crib"—so as he sees it, every child, technically, is at risk.

Until widespread trials of cord-blood treatment take place, both sides will be able to use arbitrary calculations. Those trials, alas, are probably far off: rare conditions are difficult to study on a large scale, since by definition there aren't many patients to enroll. Three years ago, Congress tried to put cord-blood trials on a faster track by expanding funds for the NIH's [National Institutes of Health's] public banks—more donations to the banks could mean more studies—but the law hasn't made much of an impact. Public banks have collected cord blood from just 105,000 babies, and fewer than 200 hospitals in the U.S. are able to draw and ship the blood to public centers. The private banks, of course, have larger stores. But they are not huge contributors to research either: only 100 of CBR's 250,000 clients have enrolled in trials thus far.

For now, parents are left to make the same speculative wager at the heart of CBR's business model: how much should you invest in science that's promising but not proven? Back in the ballroom in Tucson, the OBs [obstetricians] and midwives on the CBR junket were considering that question too. They pressed Cynthia Hextell for more details. How were the other kids in the Kurtzberg trial doing? Cynthia said the few other families she had talked to had seen improvements like Dallas's. And what risks were they warned about? "The only risk was that it wouldn't work and we would be out the money," she said. "But we just knew in our hearts that it was going to work." Other parents will have to decide whether they have that kind of faith.

EVALUATING THE AUTHORS' ARGUMENTS:

Mary Carmichael claims that media exaggerate the curative nature of embryonic stem cells. Other authors in this chapter, such as George Daley, say that iPS cells are inferior to embryonic stem cells, which remain the most powerful and promising. After reading both viewpoints, what is your opinion about the curative potential of embryonic stem cells? What swayed you?

Alternative Kinds of Stem Cell Research Can Cure Disease

David Prentice

"Non-controversial adult stem cells from bone marrow, umbilical cord blood and other tissues are treating thousands of patients around the globe."

In the following viewpoint David Prentice argues that disease can be treated and cured by alternative kinds of stem cell research. He says that although it has been touted as a miracle cure, embryonic stem cell research has yet to treat any disease. But research using adult stem cells has yielded treatments for blindness, heart failure, and organ repair from cancer damage, he says. He explains such patients have been treated using either cells from their own bodies, from donor bodies, or cells derived from the blood of the umbilical cords of newborn babies. Prentice concludes that given these developments, funding embryonic stem cell research is a waste of money and time and not worth the ethical problems it poses. He believes Americans would be better served if the government funded alternative stem cell research instead of embryonic stem cell research.

Prentice is a senior fellow for the Center for Human Life and Bioethics at the Family Research Council, a Christian nonprofit think tank and lobbying organization.

AS YOU READ, CONSIDER THE FOLLOWING QUESTIONS:
1. How did Italian doctors cure people blinded by chemical burns, as reported by Prentice?
2. What did scientists at the University of Minnesota find about the effect of adult stem cells on children with a fatal genetic skin disease, as reported by Prentice?
3. Who is Laura Dominguez and how does she factor into the author's argument?

The [August 2010] U.S. District Court injunction that stops federal taxpayer funding of human embryonic stem cell research should make patients happy. The judge ruled that federal funding for embryonic stem cell research violates a current law, passed annually since the [Bill] Clinton administration, prohibiting government funding for research that involves the destruction of human embryos.[1]

He added that there is a limited amount of federal funding for stem cells, and funding embryonic stem cells competes with adult stem cells. But only adult stem cells are treating people. The good news is that this ruling should free up more funding for adult stem cell research—which is legal, uncontroversial and already helping treat thousands of patients.

Alternative Stem Cell Treatments Work
Here are just a few examples of the published scientific successes of adult stem cells:

- Italian doctors used patients' own adult stem cells to grow new corneal tissue to restore sight to people blinded by chemical burns, including one patient who had been blind for 50 years.

1. The injunction was put on hold in September 2010 and then dropped in July 2011, once again permitting federal funding for embryonic stem cell research.

- German doctors reported in June [2010] the results of a five-year study on patients with chronic heart failure. The 191 patients treated with their own bone marrow adult stem cells showed significant improvement in heart function, with decreased death and no side effects.
- Another recent Italian success involved growing new windpipes for cancer patients. Doctors used cadaver windpipes stripped of their cells, bathed the cartilage with the patients' bone marrow stem cells and then transplanted the reconstructed windpipes. The two young women were released from the hospital just weeks after their surgery, and are now in good condition.

A technician places samples from a stem cell culture into a multiwell tray for research. Such research has yielded treatments for blindness, heart failure, and cancer-damaged organs.

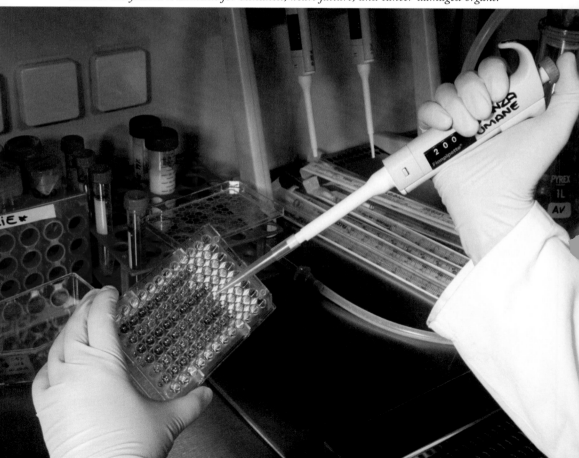

- In August [2010], University of Minnesota scientists transplanted donor adult stem cells into children with a fatal genetic skin disease and repaired the damage. The scientists said regarding adult stem cell treatments, "Patients who otherwise would have died from their disease can often now be cured. It's a serious treatment for a serious disease."

Alternatives Are Curing People Now

For sickle cell disease, published medical papers note that donor adult stem cells are the "only curative therapy." Other patients have had hip repairs using their own adult stem cells, and nonhealing bone fractures have been healed. Published medical papers in journals such as the *Journal of the American Medical Association* and *The Lancet* document improvements in patients treated with adult stem cells for juvenile diabetes and multiple sclerosis.

It is adult stem cells that are treating people now, people like Laura Dominguez. A quadriplegic after a car accident, Laura was treated for spinal-cord injury with her own nasal adult stem cells, and she has regained movement and sensation in her lower body. Laura continues to work hard at her physical therapy, bluntly stating, "I'm going to walk again."

> **FAST FACT**
>
> Adult stem cells have proved useful in developing treatments for ovarian cancer, blood cancers, diabetes, multiple sclerosis, chronic coronary artery disease, sickle-cell anemia, gangrene, liver failure, and other diseases.

Noncontroversial adult stem cells from bone marrow, umbilical cord blood and other tissues are treating thousands of patients around the globe, with an estimated 50,000 adult stem cell transplants occurring annually worldwide. For some diseases, adult stem cell transplants have become the "standard of care," meaning the treatments are so effective that they are a doctor's best choice for sick patients.

Not Worth the Controversy

Embryonic stem cells, in contrast, are ethically controversial since obtaining them requires the destruction of human embryos. However,

Adult Stem Cells Offer Treatment and Cures

Adult stem cells have yielded cures and treatments for numerous diseases, including various cancers.

Cancers:
1. Brain Cancer
2. Retinoblastoma
3. Ovarian Cancer
4. Skin Cancer: Merkel Cell Carcinoma
5. Testicular Cancer
6. Tumors Abdominal Organs Lymphoma
7. Non-Hodgkin's Lymphoma
8. Hodgkin's Lymphoma
9. Acute Lymphoblastic Leukemia
10. Acute Myelogenous Leukemia
11. Chronic Myelogenous Leukemia
12. Juvenile Myelomonocytic Leukemia
13. Chronic Myelomonocytic Leukemia
14. Cancer of the Lymph Nodes: Angioimmunoblastic Lymphadenopathy
15. Multiple Myeloma
16. Myelodysplasia
17. Breast Cancer
18. Neuroblastoma
19. Renal Cell Carcinoma
20. Soft Tissue Sarcoma
21. Various Solid Tumors
22. Ewing's Sarcoma
23. Waldenstrom's Macroglobulinemia
24. Hemophagocytic Lymphohistiocytosis
25. Poems Syndrome
26. Myelofibrosis

Autoimmune Diseases:
27. Diabetes Type I (Juvenile)
28. Systemic Lupus
29. Sjogren's Syndrome
30. Myasthenia
31. Autoimmune Cytopenia
32. Scleromyxedema
33. Scleroderma
34. Chron's Disease
35. Behcet's Disease
36. Rheumatoid Arthritis
37. Juvenile Arthritis
38. Multiple Sclerosis
39. Polychondritis
40. Systemic Vasculitis
41. Alopecia Universalis
42. Buerger's Disease

Cardiovascular:
43. Acute Heart Damage
44. Chronic Coronary Artery Disease

Ocular:
45. Corneal Regeneration

Immunodeficiencies:
46. Severe Combined Immunodeficiency Syndrome
47. X-Linked Lymphoproliferative Syndrome
48. X-Linked Hyper Immunoglobulin M Syndrome

Neural Degenerative Diseases & Injuries:
49. Parkinson's Disease
50. Spinal Cord Injury
51. Stroke Damage

Anemias & Other Blood Conditions:
52. Sickle-Cell Anemia
53. Sideroblastic Anemia
54. Aplastic Anemia
55. Red Cell Aplasia
56. Amegakaryocytic Thrombocytopenia
57. Thalassemia
58. Primary Amyloidosis
59. Diamond Blackfan Anemia
60. Fanconi's Anemia
61. Chronic Epstein-Barr Infection

Wounds and Injuries:
62. Limb Gangrene
63. Surface Wound Healing
64. Jawbone Replacement
65. Skull Bone Repair

Other Metabolic Disorders:
66. Hurler's Syndrome
67. Osteogenesis Imperfecta
68. Krabbe Leukodystrophy
69. Osteopetrosis
70. Cerebral X-Linked Adrenoleukodystrophy

Liver Disease:
71. Chronic Liver Failure
72. Liver Cirrhosis

Bladder Disease:
73. End-Stage Bladder Disease

Taken from: Do No Harm: The Coalition of Americans for Research Ethics, 2007.

millions in funding has led to no patient treatments. Adult stem cells in contrast are contained throughout the body, raising no ethical concerns.

The federal government has funded much research on adult stem cells, often for bone marrow transplants. But it can do more. Bipartisan legislation called the Patients First Act (H.R. 877), sponsored by Rep. Randy Forbes, R-Va., and Rep. Dan Lipinski, D-Ill., would prioritize federal government funding for stem cell projects that have the greatest chance for near-term benefit for patients, based on the scientific and clinical evidence.

Shouldn't we put patient treatments first? After all, it's not just tax dollars that are wasted on poor science; real lives have been lost.

EVALUATING THE AUTHORS' ARGUMENTS:

David Prentice claims that embryonic stem cell research is no longer needed now that cures have been developed using adult and induced pluripotent stem cells. In the following viewpoint George Daley argues that adult and induced pluripotent stem cells have critical limitations and thus embryonic stem cells remain crucial to stem cell research. After reading both viewpoints, what is your opinion on the importance of embryonic stem cells? Are they necessary? Why or why not? List at least two pieces of evidence that swayed you.

Viewpoint 4

Embryonic Stem Cell Research Remains Most Promising to Cure Disease

George Daley

"No matter how much progress is made with other forms of stem cells, [embryonic stem] cells will remain a vital research tool."

In the following viewpoint George Daley, in his testimony before a congressional subcommittee, argues that embryonic stem (ES) cells remain vital to stem cell research. He admits that alternatives to ES cells have treated many diseases, but ES cells remain superior to all other kinds of stem cells. Induced pluripotent stem (iPS) cells, for example, are not identical to ES cells and thus do not respond as well in certain studies. ES cells are purer and more versatile, which allows researchers to more accurately cure disease, test models, and make other scientific advances. He concludes that all forms of stem cell research have something to offer, and no one form of such research should be pursued at the expense of another. He concludes that science—and

George Daley, "Human Embryonic Stem Cells," Testimony to Senate Committee on Appropriations Subcommittee on Labor, Health and Human Services, Education, and Related Agencies, September 16, 2010. Reproduced by permission.

sick people—will be hurt if ES cell research is abandoned in favor of alternative methods.

Daley is director of the Stem Cell Transplantation Program at Children's Hospital in Boston.

AS YOU READ, CONSIDER THE FOLLOWING QUESTIONS:
1. What kind of stem cell research led to the development of induced pluripotent stem cell research, according to Daley?
2. What is *epigenetic memory,* as used by the author?
3. In what way did embryonic stem cells help researchers study Fragile X Syndrome, and why were iPS cells not as useful, in Daley's opinion?

Thank you for the invitation to testify today on the subject of human embryonic stem (ES) cells. I am here to assert that human ES cells offer unique advantages for understanding a number of human diseases and are essential to a vigorous portfolio of stem cell research here in the United States. . . .

All Kinds of Stem Cells Are Valuable

As Director of the Stem Cell Transplantation Program at Children's Hospital I speak as a doctor who uses adult stem cells to treat patients with life-threatening blood diseases—including leukemia, sickle cell anemia, immune-deficiency, bone marrow failure, and others—but I also speak as a scientist working to improve those treatments through research on adult stem cells, embryonic stem (ES) cells, and induced pluripotent stem (iPS) cells. Stem cell research is important to real live patients, and I believe to my core that stem cell research offers tremendous promise for curing a range of diseases. . . .

Opponents of ES cell research will argue that adult stem cells are more promising, that embryonic stem cells have yet to cure anyone, and that with iPS cells in hand, ES cells are no longer needed. By similar reasoning, why try to develop new classes of antibiotics? Let's just keep trying to improve penicillin. The only time I confront the argument that adult stem cells are superior to embryonic stem cells and should replace embryonic stem cells is at hearings like this. At scientific meetings, discoveries with adult and embryonic stem cells are discussed and debated as integrated and complementary aspects of cell and developmental biology, not as contestants on *American Idol*. In my opinion, such arguments are not sound scientific advice, but rather ideologically-driven attempts to prohibit scientists from using ES cells to search for new cures. No matter how much progress is made with other forms of stem cells, ES cells will remain a vital research tool, and any expulsion of ES cells from the researcher's toolkit would gravely weaken stem cell research overall.

A Continued Need for Embryonic Stem Cells

Embryonic stem cells are valuable because they are pluripotent, that is, able to make any tissue in the human body, and can grow indefinitely in a petri dish. In contrast, adult stem cells show a restricted potential for generating cells of a given tissue, and are difficult to propagate in a petri dish and thus available in limited quantities. Not all tissues regenerate from adult stem cells, which is a major reason why we need ES cells. Indeed, in juvenile diabetes, there is little or no regeneration of the insulin-producing beta cells that have been destroyed by immune attack. We are technically capable of transplanting whole pancreas or isolated pancreatic islets to replace beta cells, but there is a shortage of these organs for transplanting even the most severe diabetics. Consequently, embryonic stem cells are being developed by the biotechnology company Novocell as an alternate and more readily available source of beta cells for treatment of diabetes.

> **FAST FACT**
>
> Research on embryonic stem cells led to the discovery of less controversial induced pluripotent stem (iPS) cells, and researchers say they remain valuable for research because of their versatility and purity.

Only three years ago [in 2007], a new form of pluripotent stem cell was introduced into stem cell research, the induced pluripotent stem cell, popularly called the iPS cell. At the end of 2007, my lab was one of three world-wide to report the successful derivation of human iPS cells, and in 2008, my lab was the first to produce a repository of customized iPS cells from patients with a range of diseases

Funding for Stem Cell Research

Scientists have gained valuable treatments, cures, and knowledge from researching all kinds of stem cells, both embryonic and other. The chart below shows funding per year per type of stem cell research.

Research/ Disease Areas (dollars in millions and rounded)	Date						
	FY 2006 Actual	FY 2007 Actual	FY 2008 Actual	FY 2009 Actual	FY 2010 Actual	FY 2011 Actual	FY 2012 Actual
Stem Cell Research— Embryonic- Human	$42	$74	$88	$120	$126	$125	$128
Stem Cell Research— Embryonic- Nonhuman	$106	$120	$150	$148	$175	$175	$178
Stem Cell Research— Non-Embryonic– Human	$203	$226	$297	$339	$341	$341	$347
Stem Cell Research— Non-Embryonic– Nonhuman	$306	$400	$497	$550	$570	$569	$580
Stem Cell Research— Umbilical Cord Blood/Placenta	$22	$44	$46	$49	$42	$42	$42
Stem Cell Research— Umbilical Cord Blood/Placenta Human	$19	$38	$38	$42	$40	$40	$40
Stem Cell Research— Umbilical Cord Blood/Placenta Nonhuman	$2	$9	$9	$10	$5	$5	$5

Taken from: US Department of Health and Human Services, March 15, 2011.

like Parkinson's, diabetes, and immune deficiency. iPS cells share the defining features of ES cells—pluripotency and limitless growth, and one goal of stem cell research is to refine techniques for making iPS cells that are indistinguishable from ES cells. Thus, given that iPS cells exist, why is there a need for human ES cells, and what is the value of continued development of new human ES cell lines?

The Limitations of Non-Embryonic Stem Cells

First, it is important to note that the iPS breakthrough was founded upon the study of ES cells, and isolation of human iPS cells depended upon specific culture conditions for human, not mouse, ES cells. Today, human ES cells remain the gold standard against which our cultures of human iPS cells are compared. Human ES cells hold many more secrets, and no one can be sure where the next breakthrough will emerge.

Second, it is not clear that even ideal iPS cell lines are identical in all respects to ES cells. My lab and that of [scientist] Konrad Hochedlinger recently demonstrated that iPS cells tend to retain chemical modifications of their DNA reminiscent of their tissue of origin, so that when the iPS cells are differentiated in the petri dish, they reflect a preference to form the tissues from which they were derived. This so-called "epigenetic memory" dictates that iPS cells made from blood cells make better blood than iPS cells made from skin cells. We are working towards ways to erase these memories, but these data teach us that in practice, iPS cells harbor important differences from ES cells that influence their behavior and potential utility in research and therapy.

Embryonic Stem Cells Are More Versatile

Third, although iPS cells provide a flexible alternative to ES cells in modeling human diseases, not all diseases are readily modeled with iPS cells. One of the first diseases we attempted to model with human iPS cells was a fascinating but rare condition called Fanconi anemia that leaves kids with bone marrow failure and a predisposition to leukemia and various cancers. Despite repeated attempts, we have been unable to generate iPS cells from patients with Fanconi anemia, and last year [2009] the laboratory of Juan-Carlos Izpisua-Belmonte published that Fanconi anemia cells were resistant to iPS generation. Mice that lack the same genes as human Fanconi patients do not develop the same marrow failure and leukemia of human patients. Thus, we turned instead to modeling Fanconi anemia by depleting the relevant genes from human ES cells, and then examining the effects on human blood formation in the petri dish. Using genetically modified human ES cells, we discovered that Fanconi anemia alters the earliest stages of human embryonic blood development, teaching us that the condition develops in utero, such that children are born with stem cell deficiency, a new insight for a condition thought to develop only later in childhood.

A culture dish containing human embryos. Proponents of embryonic stem cell research say they are purer and more versatile than induced pluripotent stem cells, allowing researchers to more accurately test models and pinpoint cures for diseases, thereby more quickly advancing medical science.

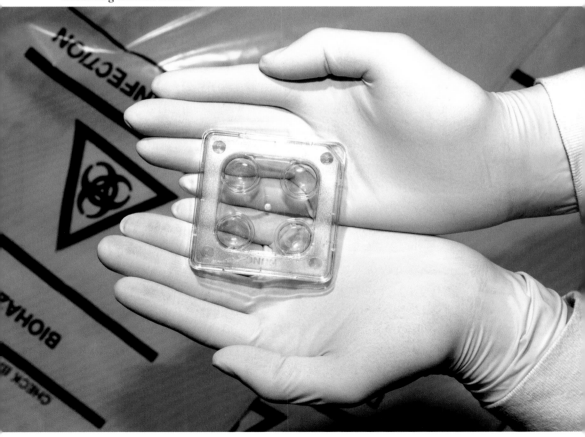

A Distinct Advantage

Another example where human ES cells offer an advantage over iPS cells is in the study of Fragile X Syndrome, the most common genetic cause of mental retardation. Fragile X is caused by a defect in the FMR1 gene, which is expressed early in human development but in affected individuals becomes aberrantly silent in adult tissues, including nerve cells. My Israeli colleague Nissim Benvenisty had generated human ES cells from discarded embryos that carried the gene defect. When these ES cells were differentiated in the petri dish, the gene shut off, just as it does during human development. In collaboration with the Benvenisty lab, we asked what would happen to the FMR1 gene in iPS cells made from skin cells of Fragile X individuals. To our surprise, the gene remained silent in iPS cells, showing that Fragile X–iPS cells differed from Fragile X–ES cells, with only the ES cells reflecting the dynamic FMR1 gene silencing observed in human development. For studying gene silencing in Fragile X, human ES cells provide a unique advantage.

Finally, human ES cells remain valuable tools for research. There is still much to be learned about human ES cells, and about how stem cells derive from human embryos. Only recently have we learned that human ES cells are markedly different from mouse ES cells, and represent a distinct type of pluripotent stem cell. Only recently have we learned that deriving human ES cells in reduced oxygen conditions preserves two active X chromosomes, which is the natural embryonic state, leaving us to question whether any of the existing human ES cells have been derived in an optimal way. When we still have so much to learn, how can we conclude that ES cells are no longer needed? . . .

Let Scientists Lead the Way

Having devoted the last 25 years of my career to aspects of adult and embryonic stem cell biology, I am convinced that human ES cells are critical to a multi-faceted portfolio of NIH [National Institutes of Health] stem cell research, and in the long run will save lives. New legislation is needed to sustain the momentum of human ES cell research in the United States, and to allow scientists—not politicians and judges—to determine which research priorities to pursue.

EVALUATING THE AUTHOR'S ARGUMENTS:

To make his argument, George Daley says that scientists—rather than politicians or judges—are the best people to make decisions about what kinds of stem cell research are most scientifically valuable. Do you agree with him? If you agree, list two reasons why scientists are better suited than others to make judgments about stem cell research. If you disagree, list two reasons why scientists may not be the best judges when it comes to stem cell research.

Media Hype Creates Unrealistic Expectations for Stem Cell Research

Sally Lehrman

"Instant miracles are uncommon in science, and journalists should do a better job making that clear."

In the following viewpoint Sally Lehrman argues that the media have hyped stem cell research and inflated Americans' ideas of what they should expect from it. She discusses California's Proposition 71, which in 2004 made billions of dollars in funding available for in-state stem cell research. Although voters had great hopes that Prop 71 would fast-track stem cell research, in reality, maintains Lehrman, this field of research is slow and arduous. The money set aside from Prop 71 helped open labs, buy equipment, and pay for other necessary research materials, but, Lehrman contends, it was unrealistic to expect that only six years later Californians would be enjoying cures coming from stem cell research. She argues that journalists must stop covering stem cell research in a dramatic way. Doing so unrealistically inflates people's understanding of what can be expected from the field. She concludes the media should cover stem cell research in a reasonable and educational way, rather than promising that cures are around the corner.

Lehrman is a science journalist and a fellow at the Markkula Center for Applied Ethics at Santa Clara University in California.

AS YOU READ, CONSIDER THE FOLLOWING QUESTIONS:
1. How much did California voters approve in funding for stem cell research in their state, according to Lehrman?
2. Who is Elaine Fuchs and how does she factor into the author's arguments?
3. Why as Lehrman tells it, did one woman insist that her dying husband be kept on a ventilator?

I t has been six years [in 2010] since California voters, awed by Proposition 71's list of potential cures for cancer, diabetes, heart disease, Alzheimer's and more than 70 other conditions, approved $3 billion in funding for stem cell research in the state. It has been nearly as long since Geron Corp. proclaimed that the first-ever human test of embryonic stem cells was nigh.

Since then, the California Institute for Regenerative Medicine, created by that 2004 ballot initiative, has handed out more than $1 billion in research funding. But there have been no "miracles"—no paralyzed people abandoning their wheelchairs or diabetics throwing away their needles. There hasn't even been a human trial of embryonic stem cells, those amazing shape-shifters that can grow into any cell in the body. In 2009, Geron almost made it into the clinic. But then mice it had treated for spinal cord injury developed worrisome cysts, and federal regulators called a halt to the pending human study.

Stem Cell Research Takes Time

So were Californians duped? Some would say yes. "There have been no cures, no therapies and little progress," *Investors Business Daily* complained in an editorial earlier this year [2010]. [Conservative radio talk show host] Rush Limbaugh went further, declaring embryonic stem cell research "fraudulent, fake."

But the truth is that science is a long and arduous process, and "breakthroughs" rest on a foundation of basic science. Most of the money spent so far has gone into new labs, training, tools and technologies and basic research, building blocks that are necessary precursors to discovery.

One day, treatments based on embryonic stem cells may be able to correct any number of life-threatening and disabling conditions. But this prospect is not a tidy matter of changing a few switches in cells and then popping them back into a malfunctioning part.

"It's very important to understand that these things won't happen quickly, nor should they," says Elaine Fuchs, who studies skin stem cells at New York's Rockefeller University. But the fundamental revelations emerging from labs here thanks to stem cell initiative funds are "incredible, exciting and inspired," she says.

Fuchs, incoming president of the International Society for Stem Cell Research, says money from the California initiative helped scientists learn how to generate pluripotent cells with much the same properties as embryonic stem cells, produce and grow both types of cells more efficiently, and understand the microenvironment of signals and internal changes that shape a cell's activity. "Really, the entire field of biology benefits," she says.

Journalists Invite Disappointment

It's no surprise that the initiative's proponents made big promises: They had something to sell. But instant miracles are uncommon in science, and journalists should do a better job making that clear. We need to highlight the uncertainties in science and, in medical quests such as stem cell therapies, emphasize the baby steps involved that in fact are big leaps: reproducing and growing these flexible cells, under-

"It's nothing that a few stem cells and 75 years of research can't fix."

standing how they work, using them to learn about disease, designing treatments and then testing the safety of any resulting therapy.

In the aftermath of the stem cell initiative, William H. Fisher, chief executive of the Alzheimer's Assn. of Northern California and Northern Nevada, found himself repeatedly having to explain such matters to hopeful families. "I don't blame the Prop. 71 people, I blame the media," he says. Alzheimer's regularly led the list of potential stem cell cures in news reports, he says, but there's no reason right now to believe that embryonic stem cells will solve the disease.

Storytellers at heart and fans of the dramatic, journalists gravitate toward the remarkable possibilities of medicine and the tragic plight of patients in need. We traffic in the language of life-saving miracles

Dr. Elaine Fuchs, president of the International Society for Stem Cell Research, says money from the state of California has helped scientists learn how to generate pluripotent stem cells with many of the same properties as embryonic stem cells. Here, she receives the National Medal of Science from President Barack Obama in 2009.

and then, for balance, throw in a dash of skepticism from a critic concerned about the sanctity of life or the exploitation of egg donors.

But science isn't a pro/con equation. When we pit enthusiastic researchers against those who cite moral objections or technical difficulties, we obscure the uncertainty that scientists themselves acknowledge. In such a context, "the belief that a cure is 'just around the corner' is able to develop and circulate," wrote sociologist Robert Evans and colleagues last year in a study of stem cell rhetoric.

By falling prey to researchers' natural enthusiasm and fixating on near-magical potential breakthroughs, journalists set us up for disappointment. In one hospital, for example, a wife insisted that her dying husband be kept on a ventilator because she was certain that stem cells could save him if he would just hang on.

Be Patient with Stem Cell Research

Despite the lack of progress in the clinic, California has benefited from the surge of research in the state, scientists say. "Stem cell funding has been an enormous stimulus for research in California," says George Q. Daley, a physician and researcher at Children's Hospital Boston, citing an impressive number of high-profile papers from labs up and down the state. Top young researchers such as Kathrin Plath, Robert Blelloch and Marius Wernig have chosen to put down stakes here. "I have to say I'm jealous," Daley says.

Any near-term boost to California's bioscience economy was waylaid by the recession, economists say. But the state did lay down an important marker as a supporter of science innovation, says Stephen Levy, senior economist for the Center for Continuing Study of the California Economy. While the payoff in new economic activity may require a few more years, he points out, "it's still true that the growth potential is enormous."

Geron, meanwhile, is back in the news, promising to start its test of a treatment for spinal cord injury later this year. And the hype is heating up anew. "A cure for paralysis is within reach," enthused an Indiana television reporter. UC [University of California] Irvine's Hans Keirstead, a Geron collaborator on the project, is "The Miracle Worker," gushed an *L.A. Times Magazine* headline writer.

Progress may indeed be in the offing, but let's not predict any wonders just yet. As a *Chicago Tribune* business writer wrote about embryonic stem cells: "All the possibilities dreamed about long ago may yet come to pass—eventually."

EVALUATING THE AUTHOR'S ARGUMENTS:

Sally Lehrman quotes from several sources to support the points she makes in her viewpoint. Make a list of everyone she quotes, including their credentials and the nature of their comments. Then, analyze her sources. Are they credible? Are they well qualified to speak on this subject? Finally, what specific points do they support?

The Media Are Biased Toward Positive Coverage of Embryonic Stem Cell Research

"The media have always been in the tank for embryonic stem cell research, often breathlessly reporting hype and spin from company [public relations] spokesmen as if it were hard news."

Wesley J. Smith

In the following viewpoint Wesley J. Smith argues that the media have unfairly favored embryonic stem (ES) cell research. He claims that American news outlets tend to enthusiastically cover good news about ES cell research while downplaying or ignoring bad news. In addition, he says that newspapers and magazines tend to overlook positive news about research using alternative kinds of stem cells, like that involving adult or induced pluripotent stem cells. He cites numerous examples of times the media hyped positive ES-related news and offers examples of times the media disregarded negative ES news or positive news about alternative stem cell research. Smith con-

Wesley J. Smith, "All the News That's Fit to Forget," *Weekly Standard*, vol. 17, is. 11, November 18, 2011.

cludes that the media's favoritism does both sick Americans and the field of journalism a disservice.

Smith is a consultant to the Center for Bioethics and Culture. He writes on many topics, from stem cell research to the death penalty to abortion.

AS YOU READ, CONSIDER THE FOLLOWING QUESTIONS:
1. What did Geron Corporation announce in November 2011, as mentioned by the author?
2. What does Smith find offensive about an October 2010 *Los Angeles Times* story titled, "Hope for Spinal Cord Patients"?
3. How did London's *Daily Telegraph* respond to a 2011 story about how adult stem cells were used to treat heart disease, according to the author, and how does he say the *New York Times, USA Today*, and the *Los Angeles Times* reacted?

For years, the media touted the promise of embryonic stem cells. Year after year, Geron Corporation announced that its embryonic stem cell treatment for acute spinal cord injury would receive FDA [Food and Drug Administration] approval "next year" for human testing. And year after year, the media dutifully informed readers and viewers that cures were imminent. When the FDA finally did approve a tiny human trial for 10 patients in January 2009, the news exploded around the world. This was it: The era of embryonic stem cell therapy had arrived!

Not exactly. Last week [in November 2011], Geron issued a terse statement announcing it was not only canceling the study, but abandoning the embryonic stem cell field altogether for financial reasons.

Biased Reporting of Stem Cell Research
You would think Geron's failure would be very big news. Instead, it turns out that the mainstream media pay attention only when embryonic stem cell research seems to be succeeding—so far, almost exclusively in animal studies. When, as here, it crashes and burns, it is scarcely news at all.

Indeed, with the laudable exception of the *Washington Post*—which outshines its competitors in reporting on biotechnology, as when it debunked the widely reported and groundless assertion that embryonic stem cell research could have cured [former president] Ronald Reagan's Alzheimer's disease—most of the same news outlets that gave Geron star treatment when it was heralding supposed breakthroughs provided only muted coverage of the company's retreat into producing anti-cancer drugs.

Media Too Quick to Applaud

The *Los Angeles Times* may be the most egregious offender. A chronic booster of Geron's embryonic stem cell research, it reported the FDA's approval of a human trial on January 24, 2009, in a story that began, "Ushering in a new era in medicine. . . ." The paper stayed on the story. In October 2010, it reported that the first patient had received an injection, then a few days later it ran a feature about the study under the headline "Hope for Spinal Cord Patients." During the same period, however, the paper did not report the encouraging results of early human trials of treatments for spinal cord injury developed using adult stem cells.

> **FAST FACT**
>
> According to a 2011 Gallup poll, 55 percent of Americans feel the media do not report news "fully, accurately, and fairly." A total 60 percent perceive bias in the media, with 47 percent believing the bias is toward a liberal point of view.

Then last May [2011], the *Times* celebrated the California Institute of Regenerative Medicine's $25 million loan to support Geron's study, noting that the company's stem cell product had performed as hoped in rat-studies. Yet the day after Geron's embryonic stem cell research unit was laid off, the *Times* couldn't find the space to print the story, though the following day a blog entry ran on the *Times* website.

Similarly, the *San Francisco Chronicle*, which had given front-page exposure to a local company when Geron's trial got underway, reported the failure of that trial in a small report on the back page of

In November 2011 the Geron Corporation announced it was abandoning embryonic stem cell research for financial reasons. Some say the research was overly hyped by the media.

the business section. The *New York Times*, always quick to applaud embryonic stem cell research, placed a small story at the bottom of page two of the business section. Other outlets carried muted reports, many focusing either on the business consequences for Geron and its stock price, or on the two other human embryonic stem cell trials currently underway, for eye conditions, run by Advanced Cell Technology.

A Double Standard for Hype and Spin

No one should be surprised by the double standard. The media have always been in the tank for embryonic stem cell research, often breathlessly reporting hype and spin from company PR [public relations] spokesmen as if it were hard news. This approach sprang largely from the media's antipathy for the pro-life movement, the most prominent opponent of research requiring the destruction of human embryos. Then there was the anti–George W. Bush prism through which science journalists and other reporters usually analyzed the issue. For nearly Bush's entire presidency, the media used people's yearning for cures as a hammer to pound the president for his decision to limit federal research funding to projects using stem cell lines already in existence and therefore not requiring the new destruction of human embryos. Rarely noted in all the criticism: During the Bush years, the NIH [National Institutes of Health] spent more than $600 million on human embryonic stem cell research.

Making matters worse, even though Bush is off the national stage, most media continue to ignore the parade of advances demonstrated in human trials of treatments relying on adult stem cells. On the very day that Geron packed its bags, for instance, the news broke of a hopeful adult stem cell treatment for heart disease. It was a big story in the United Kingdom: The headline in the *Telegraph* called it the "Biggest Breakthrough in Treating Heart Attacks for a Generation." The story noted:

> In the trial, cardiac stem cells were used to repair the severely damaged hearts of 16 patients. It was the first time this had ever been done in humans. After one year, the ejection fraction or "pumping efficiency" of the hearts of eight patients had improved by more than 12 percent. All patients whose progress was followed underwent some level of recovery. . . . Although this was an early stage trial and larger studies are needed, scientists believe the promise it shows has huge implications.

How did the *New York Times* report this story? It didn't. The *L.A. Times?* A blog entry. *USA Today?* Nada. *San Francisco Chronicle?* At least it was in the paper— on page A16, under the hardly descriptive headline "Regimen Shown To Aid Heart Patients." And so it goes.

Unfair Coverage

Imagine if a human trial using *embryonic* stem cells had shown improvement to damaged human hearts. You can just see the banner headline in the *New York Times* and the breathless announcements on the network news. The thought experiment makes blatantly obvious the malpractice that plagues reporting in this field—which is doubly regrettable, since not only are editors and reporters undermining the media's already tarnished reputation for objectivity, but many suffering people and their families still have not heard the hopeful news generated by the ethical exploration of regenerative medicine.

EVALUATING THE AUTHOR'S ARGUMENTS:

Wesley J. Smith argues that the media favor positive stories about embryonic stem cell research. How do you think each of the other authors represented in this chapter would respond to this claim? For each author, write one or two sentences on how they might respond. Then, state with which author(s) you are most likely to agree, and why.

Chapter 3

To What Extent Should the Government Support Stem Cell Research?

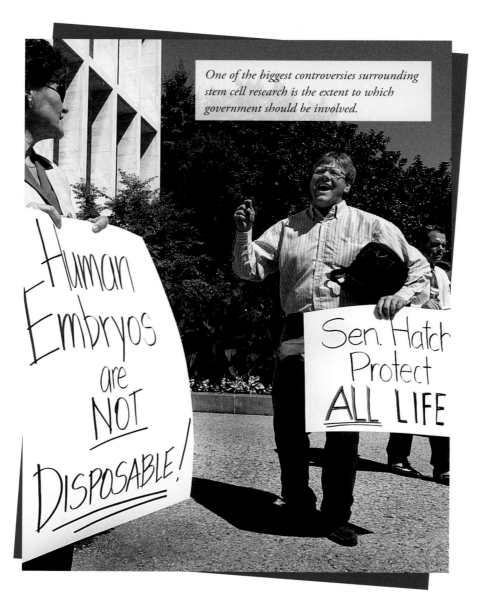

One of the biggest controversies surrounding stem cell research is the extent to which government should be involved.

The Government Should Fund Embryonic Stem Cell Research

"Embryonic stem cells have the potential to be turned into different kinds of tissue that could be used to regenerate and repair tissue and treat a host of diseases including heart disease, Parkinson's, diabetes and Lou Gehrig's disease."

Jim Abrams

Jim Abrams is a writer for the Associated Press. In the following viewpoint Abrams discusses a Democratic senator's belief that the government should fund embryonic stem cell research. The senator laments that recent court rulings have disrupted embryonic stem cell research, and warns that cutting off funding would deliver a devastating blow to this promising field of research. Government involvement in stem cell research is the best way to make sure it takes place ethically, he suggests, and government has the responsibility to invest in the cures of the future.

1. What are some examples of the diseases embryonic stem cell research has promise in curing?
2. How much money has the National Institutes of Health spent on embryonic stem cell research, as cited in the article?
3. Does NIH director Francis S. Collins believe stem cell research is beneficial?

A leading Democratic senator said Thursday that Congress should "get busy" on giving legal stature to U.S. government funding of human embryonic stem cell research to avoid giving a final say on the issue to a conservative Supreme Court.

Sen Arlen Specter spoke at a Senate hearing where scientists also expressed concern about recent court rulings that have disrupted funding for embryonic stem cell research, seen as offering promising potential for treating Parkinson's Disease, spinal cord injuries and numerous other debilitating illnesses.

FAST FACT

Just 20 percent of Americans said stem cell research would be an extremely important factor in whom they elect as president, according to a 2007 CNN/Opinion Research Corporation poll. Terrorism, education, health care, gas prices, corruption, the economy, illegal immigration, global warming, and abortion were among the issues that took greater priority.

"Congress had better get busy and had better act on this subject so we do not wait for court action," said Specter, who earlier this week introduced legislation to codify rules issues by President Barack Obama last year to ease restrictions on embryonic stem cell research.

He cited several recent cases where the Supreme Court had issued stays on lower court rulings on "ideological grounds."

Sen. Tom Harkin, a Democrat and head of the Senate Appropriations health subcommittee that held the hearing, concurred. "We've come too far to give up now," he said. "If we don't win this battle now we'll have to take it up in Congress." Harkin too has introduced legislation to allow for federal funding of human embryonic stem cell research.

The National Institutes of Health has already spent more than $500 million on this research, proceeding with federal funding since President George W. Bush in 2001 allowed restricted federal assistance.

But last month U.S. District Court Judge Royce Lamberth issued a preliminary injunction in which he stated that the research violated a 1996 law banning the use of taxpayer money to derive stem cells from embryos. An appeals court has since temporarily stayed that order until it can hear full arguments in the coming weeks.

Americans Think the Government Should Fund Embryonic Stem Cell Research

A 2010 Gallup poll found that the majority of Americans think the government should provide funding for stem cell research that involves human embryos. Democrats are more likely to support embryonic stem cell research than Independents or Republicans.

Question: "Do you think the federal government should or should not fund research that would use newly created stem cells obtained from human embryos?"

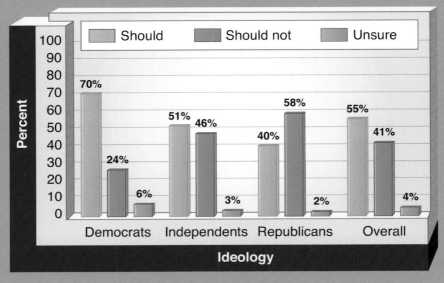

Taken from: CNN/Opinion Research Corporation Poll, September 1–2, 2010.

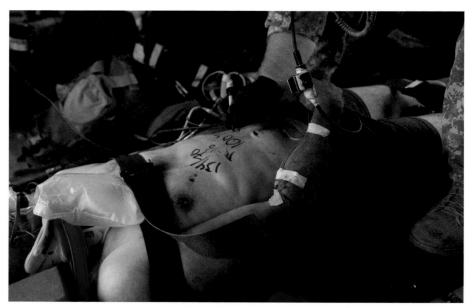

Wounded US soldiers have received blood transfusions of lab-made blood generated from stem cells.

Uncertainty Created in Embryonic Stem Cell Research

Despite that temporary reprieve, the injunction "has created deep uncertainty in the field of embryonic stem cell research," testified NIH director Francis S. Collins. He said 244 pending grants adding up to about $200 million had to be put on hold. To have funding cut off "would be a devastating blow."

George Q. Daley, associate director of the stem cell program at Children's Hospital Boston, said doubts about court action are "disrupting our research, they are dissuading scientists from entering the field and they are threatening American preeminence in the research." Embryonic stem cells have the potential to be turned into different kinds of tissue that could be used to regenerate and repair tissue and treat a host of diseases including heart disease, Parkinson's, diabetes and Lou Gehrig's disease. The cells are derived from excess embryos created during in vitro fertilization therapies that would eventually be discarded.

Opponents say the research is another form of abortion because human embryos must be destroyed to obtain the stem cells.

Sen. Roger Wicker, a Republican and co-author of the 1996 law prohibiting the use of federal funds in work that harms an embryo, said at the hearing that the emphasis should be put on using adult stem cells for research, thus avoiding the "ethical challenges" associated with embryonic cells.

As a result of that law, government policy has been to work with stem cells after private money is used to cull them from embryos.

Collins said the NIH [currently] spends more on adult stem cell research than on embryonic stem cells, but that the two types of cells have different potential and current uses in both areas must be pursued.

EVALUATING THE AUTHOR'S ARGUMENTS:

Jim Abrams relays beliefs that federal funding for embryonic stem cell research would be beneficial. What is your opinion of this approach to the issue? What points made by Abrams strengthen this view?

The Private Sector Should Fund Stem Cell Research

"Medical research would not wither away if the government took a back seat to the private sector."

Jeff Jacoby

In the following viewpoint Jeff Jacoby argues that the private sector is a better source of funding for embryonic stem (ES) cell research than the government. He explains that the original ES cell research was funded with private moneys, and many of the current breakthroughs and advancements are paid for with contributions from corporations and charities. Jacoby says government funding can be fickle—decisions by judges stop and start funding erratically, and the fact that ES research is controversial makes it beholden to public opinion. Jacoby says given the fact that private sources are more than willing to fund ES research, there is no real need to involve the government.

Jacoby is a reporter for the *Boston Globe*.

AS YOU READ, CONSIDER THE FOLLOWING QUESTIONS:

1. Who funded James Thomson's research, according to Jacoby?
2. Name at least three corporations Jacoby says have funded stem cell research.
3. How much did philanthropist Eli Broad and Ray Dolby give stem cell researchers, as reported by the author?

James Thomson, an embryologist at the University of Wisconsin, cultivated the first embryonic stem cell lines in 1998. By then the prohibition on using federal funds for scientific research in which human embryos are destroyed was already on the books; President Bill Clinton had signed it nearly three years earlier. So how did Thomson secure a government grant to finance his landmark achievement?

A Way Around the Law

He didn't. His work was funded by the Geron Corporation, a California Biotechnology company that develops treatments for cancer, spinal cord injuries, and degenerative diseases. Thomson was scrupulous about obeying the congressional ban, known as the Dickey-Wicker amendment. The *Washington Post* reported that he did his research "in a room in which not a single piece of equipment, not even an electrical extension cord, had been bought with federal funds."

Scientists and the government subsequently found a way around the Dickey-Wicker amendment—they interpreted it as applying only to the destruction of human embryos required to extract stem cells, not to the research conducted afterward. So while the National Institutes of Health [NIH] could not fund the actual cultivation of embryonic stem-cell lines, it could funnel taxpayer dollars to scientists experimenting with those lines. Last year [in 2009], NIH provided $143 million for embryonic stem-cell research.

Federally Funded Fits and Starts

But last week [in August 2010] a federal judge in Washington pronounced that before/after distinction meaningless. Dickey-Wicker "unambiguously" prohibits the use of federal funds for *all* research in which a human embryo is destroyed, Judge Royce Lamberth ruled, "not just the 'piece of research' in which the embryo is destroyed." His injunction temporarily blocking the [Barack] Obama administration from expanding funding of embryonic stem-cell research has thrown the field into turmoil. Some 85 grant applications in the NIH pipeline have been stopped in their tracks.[1]

1. The injunction was put on hold in September 2010 and then dropped in July 2011, once again permitting federal funding for embryonic stem cell research.

Naturally, the ruling was condemned by supporters of embryonic stem-cell experimentation—*The New York Times* labeled it "a serious blow to medical research"—while activists who oppose the harvesting of human embryos on moral grounds rejoiced.

To my mind, there is no moral obstacle to using leftover fertility-clinic embryos that would otherwise be discarded for medical research. Nor do I regard a microscopic cluster of cells as a human person entitled to full legal protection. Nevertheless, Lamberth's ruling makes this a good moment to ask a threshold question: Why should the federal government be funding controversial medical research in the first place?

Government Money Not Needed

As Thomson's 1998 discovery proved, pathbreaking accomplishments in stem-cell science are possible even when the government isn't footing the bill. That was no anomaly. If the feds didn't fund the search for embryonic stem-cell therapies, the private sector would.

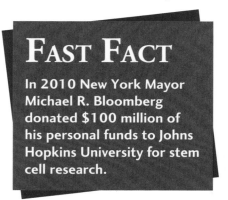

FAST FACT

In 2010 New York Mayor Michael R. Bloomberg donated $100 million of his personal funds to Johns Hopkins University for stem cell research.

As it is, a host of private funders are already pouring money into stem-cell research. Just last month [in July 2010], Geron, the company that underwrote Thomson's work in 1998, announced plans to conduct the world's first human clinical trial of a therapy derived from embryonic stem cells, a treatment for damaged spinal cords. And Geron is only one of many corporations—Aastrom Biosciences, Stemcells Inc., and Osiris Therapeutics are among the others—using private dollars to fund cutting-edge stem-cell research.

Private Funding Is Stable and Consistent

For-profit corporations and their shareholders aren't the only source of private-sector stem-cell funding. The *Washington Post* reported in 2006 on the private philanthropy that was building new stem-cell labs

Los Angeles philanthropist Eli Broad (pictured) gave $25 million to the University of Southern California for a stem cell institute. Many other philanthropists have also given funds for stem cell research.

in academia. "Los Angeles philanthropist Eli Broad gave $25 million to the University of Southern California for a stem cell institute, sound-technology pioneer Ray Dolby gave $16 million to the University of California at San Francisco, and local donors are contributing to a $75 million expansion at the University of California at Davis. . . . Early

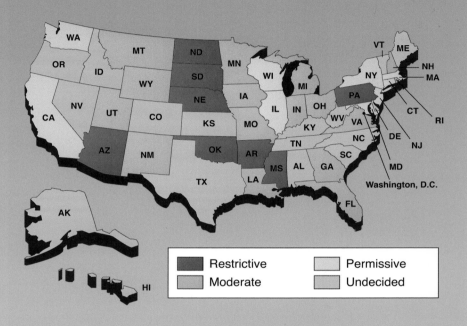

State Stem Cell Policies

Some states have set aside billions of dollars to fund stem cell research, while others have specifically prohibited the use of public money for such a purpose. Private companies and charities have made large donations to labs and facilities in the more permissive states.

Legend:
- Restrictive
- Moderate
- Permissive
- Undecided

Taken from: James A. Baker III. "Stem Cell Policy In the Obama Age: Texas, U.S., and U.K. Perspectives." Institute for Public Policy, September 2009, p. 15.

this year [2010,] New York Mayor Michael R. Bloomberg quietly donated $100 million to Johns Hopkins University, largely for stem-cell research."

Add to them the Starr Foundation, the Juvenile Diabetes Research Foundation, the Michael J. Fox Foundation, and all the other private charities that have made stem-cell research a priority. Imagine those that would do so if the federal government stopped underwriting research that so many taxpayers find problematic.

Douglas Melton, the co-director of Harvard's Stem Cell Institute, told the *Boston Globe* last week that private support is "the only durable and consistent source" of funding for embryonic stem-cell research. He's right. Medical research would not wither away if the government took a back seat to the private sector. In this, as in so many other areas, perhaps it's time to re-think Washington's role.

EVALUATING THE AUTHOR'S ARGUMENTS:

Given what you know on this topic, list three reasons the government should fund stem cell research and three reasons the government should not fund stem cell research. What benefits come from involving the government in the funding and oversight of this field? What drawbacks are there? After considering both positions, state your opinion on whether the government should fund such research.

The Government Must Create Ethical Guidelines for Stem Cell Research

Kristen Matthews

"Current regulation of stem cell research in the United States is, at best, haphazard, with [some] scientists . . . playing by a different set of rules."

The government should create a comprehensive, federal stem cell policy that would apply to all researchers, argues Kristen Matthews in the following viewpoint. She explains that because not all stem cell research is publicly funded, it has not been universally regulated. As a result, different researchers follow different rules and regulations in their research. But Matthews explains that embryonic stem (ES) cell research is a very sensitive endeavor, one that must be governed by a carefully crafted set of ethical guidelines. She says that if the government is going to fund such cell research, it must craft a responsible and thorough policy that will unify researchers going forward.

Matthews is a fellow in science and technology policy at the Baker Institute for

Public Policy at Rice University in Texas. Part of her job includes managing the activities of the Science and Technology Policy Program, including the institute's International Stem Cell Policy Program.

AS YOU READ, CONSIDER THE FOLLOWING QUESTIONS:
1. Why, according to Matthews, were researchers at Harvard University and the University of Wisconsin–Madison not required to follow federally crafted rules for stem cell research?
2. What kind of stem cell research guidelines does the author say the National Academies put forth in 2005?
3. What does ESCRO stand for and how does it factor into Matthews's viewpoint?

With Barack Obama in the Oval Office, opportunities for human embryonic stem cell research are expected to increase dramatically. Our new president has promised to back legislation that would allow federal funding of additional stem cells—a move that has been welcomed by scientists across the globe.

But allowing expanded research is only one part of U.S. leadership in this important area of biomedical research. President Obama should also act to develop a broader, comprehensive federal stem cell policy that ensures stem cell research is conducted in a responsible, thoughtful and ethical manner that restores the federal government's essential role in oversight of this critical subject.

A Delicate Matter

Human embryonic stem cell research focuses on the cells derived from five- to six-day-old fertilized eggs. Unlike adult stem cells, which are specialized to particular tissues or organs, embryonic stem cells have the potential to specialize into any cell in the body and therefore have the capability to be utilized in tissues and organs where stem cells are missing or damaged. Advocates predict that embryonic stem cells could be used to produce tissues or organs to replace damaged ones, to understand and combat diseases such as diabetes and Parkinson's, and to test and develop new drugs.

The field is relatively new, dating back just over a decade, and the need for strong ethical guidelines and coordination is increasingly apparent. Unfortunately, current regulation of stem cell research in the United States is, at best, haphazard, with scientists who accept state and private funding on cells playing by a different set of rules than researchers using government cells.

Different Sets of Rules Exist

In 2001, President George W. Bush restricted federal funding for stem cell research, severely limiting the amount and scope of research. But the restriction applied only to federal funding. So some universities, including Harvard University and the University of Wisconsin–Madison, obtained private funding for their research. Other researchers convinced legislators and governors in states such as California, Illinois and Connecticut to fund projects.

California Republican governor Arnold Schwarzenegger and Democratic senator from California Dianne Feinstein worked together in 2005 to pass legislation that allowed human embryonic stem cell research but banned human cloning.

In the absence of federal oversight and coordination, the National Academies stepped in with voluntary guidelines in 2005—but there was no mechanism to ensure these practices are followed. Additionally, as the federal government has pulled back from stem cell research, the United States' leadership role in this area has diminished, with research here stagnating compared to the rest of the world.

A Comprehensive Policy Is Needed

To rectify this, the Obama administration should create a comprehensive federal stem cell policy

> ## FAST FACT
>
> Stem cell research is conducted in Australia, Belgium, Brazil, Canada, China, the Czech Republic, Denmark, Estonia, Finland, France, Greece, Hong Kong, Hungary, Iceland, India, Iran, Israel, Japan, Latvia, the Netherlands, New Zealand, Portugal, Russia, Singapore, Slovenia, South Africa, South Korea, Spain, Sweden, Switzerland, Taiwan, Thailand, Turkey, the United Kingdom, and the United States.

with the National Institutes of Health (NIH) taking the lead. This could be done by creating an Embryonic Stem Cell Research Oversight (ESCRO) board within the NIH to review controversial research and recommend policy for the agency, similar to the committee recommended by the National Academies, the most distinguished society of scientists and engineers in the country.

The ESCRO board would contain representatives with expertise in ethical and legal issues and biology, as well as policy scholars and patient advocates. The role of the board should be to review grant applications and to develop policy options for all aspects of research involving human embryos. Moreover, NIH should work with states that have already implemented human stem cell programs to provide guidance on ethics and research, as well as to help with peer review.

Banning Human Cloning

The government must also outlaw any effort to clone a human being, regardless of the source of funding. Human reproductive cloning has been

Stem Cell Research Around the World

Stem cell research policies vary around the world. Some worry that the most permissive countries lack ethical research guidelines.

"Permissive" = various embryonic stem cell derivation techniques, including somatic cell nuclear transfer (SCNT), also called research or therapeutic cloning. SCNT is the transfer of a cell nucleus from a somatic, or body, cell into an egg from which the nucleus has been removed.

"Flexible" = derivations from fertility clinic donations only, excluding SCNT, and often under certain restrictions.

Restrictive policy or no established policy. Restrictive policies range from outright prohibition of human embryo research to permitting research on imported embryonic stem cell lines only to permitting research on a limited number of previously established stem cell lines.

● The black dots show the locations of some of the leading genome sequencing research centers. Most US centers are those that have been involved in the Human Genome Project.

Map is designed to reflect national policy and whether or not public funds may be used to pursue stem cell research using in vitro fertilization (IVF) embryos donated from fertility clinics.

denounced by scientists and policymakers around the world. Fourteen states and more than 40 countries have already banned the practice.

This increased federal involvement reflects public sentiment. Public support for stem cell research has increased over the past seven years, with 56 percent of Americans supporting federal funding according to Research!America. And approximately two-thirds of Americans agree that there should be a uniform federal stem cell policy.

There is also a historical precedent for an empowered NIH. In the past, NIH has played a strong leadership role in creating research policy for controversial areas of biomedical research. For example, the Recombinant DNA Advisory Committee (RAC) was created to review proposals involving the use of DNA in research and clinical therapies.

Thoughtful, Ethical, and Uniform Guidelines

Additionally, President Obama should continue the President's Council on Bioethics (PCB) and provide it with a mandate, along with the necessary financial support, to guide the president on bioethical questions as well as serve as a means for public outreach on these topics.

These steps are critical if the United States is to resume its leadership role in scientific research and help establish global standards that reflect scientists' interests while respecting human dignity.

Let's hope our new president takes this opportunity to promote a federal stem cell policy that expands research in a responsible, thoughtful and ethical manner.

EVALUATING THE AUTHOR'S ARGUMENTS:

In this viewpoint, Kristen Matthews uses facts, examples, and history to make her argument that the government must create ethical guidelines for stem cell research. She does not, however, use any quotations to support her point. If you were to rewrite this article and insert quotations, what authorities might you quote from? Where would you place the quotations, and why?

The United States Has Fallen Behind in Stem Cell Research

Jonathan D. Moreno and Sam Berger

"U.S. stem cell policy hurts American competitiveness and slows international research."

In the following viewpoint, Jonathan D. Moreno and Sam Berger warn that restrictive embryonic stem [ES] cell research policies have caused the US to lag behind other countries. They claim that former President George W. Bush crippled US researchers when he restricted federal funding to just a handful of existing stem cell lines. Although President Barack Obama has since loosened restrictions, federal funding is still unavailable for new lines created from embryos, and many research processes are overly time-consuming and bureaucratic. The authors regret that many more ES cell lines are available to British researchers, and note that other countries, like Singapore, have enviably open policies that allow researchers to more easily advance their work. Moreno and Berger conclude that the US needs to

This material 'Minding the Stem Cell Gap' by Jonathan D. Moreno and Same Berger, October 23, 2006 was created by the Center for American Progress (www.americanprogress.org). Reproduced by permission.

promote greater acceptance of ES cell research if its researchers are to remain internationally competitive.

Moreno is a senior fellow and Berger a researcher at the Center for American Progress, a progressive and liberal policy organization.

AS YOU READ, CONSIDER THE FOLLOWING QUESTIONS:
1. What percent of state funding for stem cell research has gone to resources other than actual research, according to the authors?
2. What do Moreno and Berger say happened to the number of stem cell publications by U.S. researchers between 2002 and 2004?
3. Where is the Biopolis located, and how does it factor into the authors' argument?

U.S. stem cell policy hurts American competitiveness and slows international research. American scientists are forced to work with old, contaminated stem cell lines, while scientists around the world use the latest lines to speed up their work and close the research gap. This restrictive U.S. policy makes collaboration with foreign scientists more difficult and means a large amount of worldwide funding for stem cell research is being used on less useful lines. Updating the American stem cell policy to allow federally funded scientists to use the best research tools would both aid research internationally and improve U.S. competitiveness.

> **FAST FACT**
>
> The Georgia Institute of Technology reported in 2008 that permissive public policies and generous public funding helped the United Kingdom, Israel, China, Singapore and Australia produce a wealth of embryonic stem cell research.

Our restrictive federal stem cell policy hampers international research. Science is a collaborative process; research discoveries by one group of scientists often provide the basis for advances in laboratories around the world. The U.S. is by far the largest funder of stem cell

National Institutes of Health director Francis Collins testifies before the US Senate that cutting off funding for embryonic stem cell research would cause irreparable harm to researchers, taxpayers, and scientific progress.

research, spending three times as much as any other country, and state funding in the U.S. also exceeds that of most other countries.

But federal funding goes to only 21 older stem cell lines that are of limited use for research. And our federal policy forces states that want to allow researchers to use newer, federally ineligible stem cell lines to waste resources on new infrastructure and equipment; 86 percent of state funding for stem cell research has gone to building infrastructure, purchasing equipment, and training scientists, not to actual research.

The federal stem cell policy also makes it difficult for other countries to collaborate with the United States, because their scientists are working with newer lines that are ineligible for our federal funding. Home to the top facilities in the world, the U.S. has traditionally been an important research hub. Yet restrictive federal policies make international scientists less eager to work with federally funded scientists, even though there is greater available funding from the National Institutes of Health. The international community recognizes the damage that the U.S. policy causes to international efforts. The International Society for Stem Cell Research strongly supported recent legislation that President Bush vetoed that would have allowed federal funding for research using newer stem cell lines.

The U.K., which frequently collaborates with the U.S., has even bypassed the federal government in favor of forming ties with the

Americans Worry the United States Will Fall Behind

About half of all Americans expressed concern that their country would lag behind others due to a lack of government support for stem cell research.

Question: If the federal government does not fund stem cell research from human embryos, the United States will fall behind other countries in terms of leadership in the development of new drugs and preventing diseases.

2010

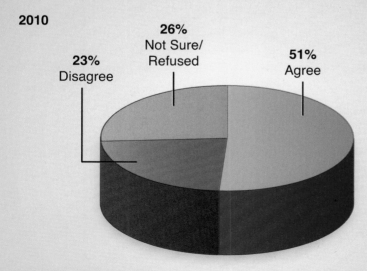

26%
Not Sure/
Refused

23%
Disagree

51%
Agree

Taken from: Harris Interactive, 2010.

International Attitudes on Stem Cell Research

Americans are more supportive of embryonic stem cell research than people are in places like Ireland, Germany, or Greece, but less supportive than residents of places like Iceland, Norway, and Sweden.

Country	Do not forbid	Forbid	Do Not know or refused to answer
Iceland	71%	25%	5%
Norway	69%	25%	6%
Sweden	67%	28%	6%
Britain	65%	27%	8%
Netherlands	63%	34%	4%
Belgium	62%	33%	5%
Czech Republic	62%	31%	7%
United States	60%	31%	9%
Denmark	58%	39%	4%
Finland	58%	34%	8%
France	58%	32%	9%
Spain	58%	32%	10%
Northern Ireland	53%	32%	15%
Hungary	51%	42%	7%
Italy	50%	38%	12%
Switzerland	49%	41%	10%
Lithuania	49%	32%	19%
Ireland	46%	33%	21%
Germany	45%	49%	7%
Estonia	45%	33%	22%
Latvia	44%	45%	11%
Poland	44%	42%	14%
Slovakia	43%	49%	7%
Croatia	43%	42%	15%
Portugal	42%	40%	18%
Slovenia	41%	54%	5%
Cyprus (Republic)	41%	41%	18%
Malta	41%	37%	22%
Greece	39%	54%	7%
Bulgaria	39%	34%	27%
Luxembourg	38%	54%	8%
Turkey	38%	42%	20%
Romania	38%	36%	26%
Austria	33%	60%	7%

Taken from: Robert J. Blendon, Minah Kang Kim, and John M. Benson. "The Public, Political Parties, and Stem-Cell Research." *New England Journal of Medicine*, November 17, 2011, p. 1855.

California Institute for Regenerative Medicine, the body that oversees stem cell research in the state. Prime Minister Blair is interested in working with CIRM because he thinks the U.K. can more effectively collaborate with California scientists than researchers who receive only federal funding, and because he believes he can lure private U.S. stem cell firms to Britain. The U.S. stem cell policy has relegated the federal government to second place status in its own country.

While the U.S. lags, others countries are rushing to fill the research gap. The number of stem cell publications by U.S. researchers decreased from roughly 33 percent to around 25 percent between 2002 and 2004. Sensing an opportunity, other countries have begun to focus strongly on supporting stem cell research; the U.S. greatly outspends the U.K. on stem cell research in total dollars, but the U.K. devotes a larger percentage of its overall bioscience funding to stem cells. These countries also have created more progressive stem cell policies that support research using a wide variety of stem cell lines.

Singapore, a country with a much smaller national budget than the U.S., has taken substantial steps to support stem cell research. The country has built a $300 million biomedical research facility called the Biopolis, has announced that it will spend $7.5 billion on biomedical research over the next five years, and is actively courting U.S. stem cell researchers. This support has paid off; the Biopolis has already attracted major U.S. stem cell researchers from the National Cancer Institute, MIT, and the University of California. A biotech company in Singapore was also the first to announce the derivation of stem cell lines that meet clinical use standards for humans, a breakthrough that promises to speed up research and be quite profitable.

The U.S. is losing ground in stem cell research, but the outlook is not wholly grim. America still outspends other countries on research, and has a research infrastructure that is the most effective in the world at transforming new discoveries into clinical applications. Yet the U.S. must act quickly to support stem cell research on par with international competitors. The biggest threat is not just that current research and collaborative efforts with other countries will be hampered, but also that potential future American stem cell researchers will be discouraged from entering the field, leading to a far greater stem cell research gap in the future. A rising tide lifts all laboratories, but if the U.S. does not update its stem cell policy soon, it may miss the boat.

EVALUATING THE AUTHORS' ARGUMENTS:

The authors of this viewpoint say that in order to remain competitive, the US must increase funding for ES cell research and increase the number of ES cell lines on which research can be performed. However, doing so would require embryos to be destroyed, an ethically controversial event. If you were to write guidelines for this process, what might they include? Would you allow discarded IVF embryos to be donated to researchers? Would you allow researchers to clone new embryos? Would you not allow any new lines to be created, claiming that the existing ones are sufficient? Explain your position given what you know on the topic.

The United States Has Not Fallen Behind in Stem Cell Research

New Scientist

"US research on [human embryonic stem cells] leaves others trailing."

In the following viewpoint, editors at the magazine *New Scientist* contend that the American embryonic stem (ES) cell research industry is in good health. They argue that policies put in place by former president George W. Bush have not hampered researchers or caused them to lag behind researchers in other countries. As of 2011, they note, the majority of papers mentioning human ES cells had at least one American author. Importantly, the first clinical trials of such research have taken place in the United States, too. The editors admit there are some kinds of research and trials that the United States has pursued less aggressively than other countries, but in these cases they have proceeded with caution out of respect for human life, not as a result of restrictive policies. They conclude that the United States remains the leader in ES cell research and that former president Bush's policies did not hinder research.

AS YOU READ, CONSIDER THE FOLLOWING QUESTIONS:
1. In what percentage of papers mentioning human embryonic stem cells in 2011 do the editors say had at least one US-based author?
2. What percentage of such papers had UK-based authors, as mentioned by *New Scientist*'s editors?
3. Who is Jesse Gelsinger and how does he factor into the authors' argument?

The stem cell revolution is finally under way. South Korea has approved the first commercial treatment for heart attack victims, while in Sweden a patient has been given an artificial windpipe coated with his own cells.

These developments and others are welcome, but they hint that the US, the world's research powerhouse, is lagging behind in bringing stem cell treatments to the masses. If that's the case, it is tempting to blame President George W. Bush's restrictions on research using human embryonic stem cells (hESCs). Tempting, but misplaced.

US Leadership in Stem Cell Research

A *New Scientist* analysis based on research papers from this year [2011] indicates that US research on hESCs leaves others trailing: 45 per cent of 204 papers mentioning hESCs had at least one US-based author; UK scientists were a distant second, with 17 per cent. On top of that, the first trials of hESC-based treatments are taking place in the US.

It is also worth noting that the heart treatment and windpipe

> **FAST FACT**
>
> Research on all kinds of stem cells continues to grow in the United States The journal *Cell* reports that in 2008, 15, or 5.1 percent, of research papers on stem cells reported work using adult stem cells, and just three papers combined both adult and embryonic stem cell research. By 2010, 161 of 574 papers, or 28 percent, reported on studies of both research types, and 62.1 percent of those papers looked at both induced and embryonic cell lines.

implant do not use hESCs but adult mesenchymal stem cells, which were not subject to Bush's restrictions. Our analysis shows that the US also leads in research papers in this field—although not by so much.

Exercising Reasonable Caution

Yet the US does seem to lag in one key respect. Our search of the ClinicalTrials.gov database for a random sample of 30 clinical trials using these adult stem cells yielded seven in China, six in South Korea, and just three in the US. Why? Again, don't blame Bush. The low number reflects the prudence of the US Food and Drug Administration [FDA], which approves trials. While the agency is often criticised by patient-advocates for its conservative attitude, two words justify its caution: Jesse Gelsinger.

The 18-year-old died in 1999 after an experimental therapy. If a similar tragedy were to befall a stem cell trial, it could stymie the field, as Gelsinger's death did to gene therapy. The FDA is wise to be cautious. Bush's restrictions may not have had the expected effect, but uncertainty still prevails: a current lawsuit could yet stall federal funding to hESCs. Nevertheless, those who would restrict the research must now accept that progress is unstoppable.

In Sweden, a patient receives a new trachea grown from his own stem cells.

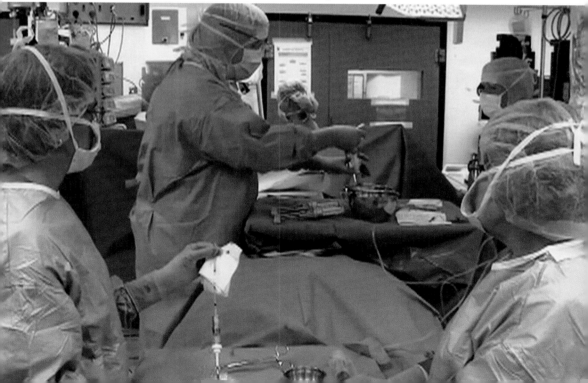

United States Leads in Worldwide Embryonic Stem Cell Research

The *New Scientist* searched a scientific database for research papers published in 2011 mentioning various types of stem cells. It found that the United States enjoys a dominant position in research on embryonic stem cells and induced pluripotent stem cells (iPSCs). The United States also leads in work on adult mesenchymal stem cells and on RNA interference, although to a smaller degree.

Search Term	"Human embryonic stem cell"
1st US	45.1% of papers had at least one US-based author
2nd United Kingdom	16.7%

Search Term	"Human induced pluripotent stem cell"
1st US	52.3%
2nd Japan	15.9%

Search Term	"Human mesenchymal stem cell"
1st US	26.8%
2nd South Korea	14.2%

Search Term	"Embryonic stem cell"
1st US	45.4%
2nd China	12.8%

Search Term	"Induced pluripotent stem cell"
1st US	51.7%
2nd Japan	17.6%

Search Term	"Mesenchymal stem cell"
1st US	29.5%
2nd China	20.1%

Search Term	"RNA Interference"
1st US	36.8%
2nd China	26.6%

Taken from: *New Scientist.* "US Stem Cell Research in Robust Health Supplementary Analysis," July 13, 2011. www.newscientist.com/article/mg21128212.800-us-stem-cell-research-in-robust-health.html.

New Scientist searched the Web of Science [a database] for research papers published in 2011 mentioning various types of stem cell. For comparison with another leading biotechnology, we also searched for papers mentioning RNA interference. The results indicate that the US enjoys a dominant position in research on embryonic stem cells (ESCs) and similarly versatile induced pluripotent stem cells (iPSCs). The US also leads in work on adult mesenchymal stem cells and on RNA interference, although by smaller margins. . . .

Searches back to 2000 also suggest that the US contribution to work on human embryonic stem cells has stayed at roughly the same proportional level over the past decade.

US Dominance Remains

To our knowledge, only three clinical trials involving treatments derived from human ESCs have been approved, all in the US; therapies derived from iPSCs have not yet entered clinical trials.

Our analysis of searches at ClinicalTrials.gov suggests that some other countries are moving more quickly than the US into trials of novel therapies involving mesenchymal stem cells. This seems to reflect regulatory caution on the part of the US Food and Drug Administration. The US dominates the listings for current trials on blood stem cells, which have been in clinical use for many years. Here, the risks are better understood and FDA approval is easier to obtain.

EVALUATING THE AUTHORS' ARGUMENTS:

The authors of this viewpoint use the number of published papers with US authors as a measure for demonstrating that the United States remains competitive in stem cell research. The authors of the previous viewpoint use the number of available stem cell lines as a measure for demonstrating that the United States has fallen behind other countries in stem cell research. Which do you think is a better measure of American competitiveness—the number of published papers or number of available stem cell lines? Why?

Facts About Stem Cell Research

Editor's note: These facts can be used in reports or papers to reinforce or add credibility when making important points or claims.

The Morality of Stem Cell Research

A 2011 Gallup poll found opinions about stem cell research have become slightly more favorable over time:

- In 2011, 62 percent of Americans viewed stem cell research as morally acceptable; 30 percent viewed it as morally wrong.
- In 2010, 59 percent viewed it as morally acceptable; 32 percent viewed it as morally wrong.
- In 2009, 57 percent viewed it as morally acceptable; 36 percent viewed it as morally wrong.
- In 2008, 62 percent viewed it as morally acceptable; 30 percent viewed it as morally wrong.
- In 2007, 64 percent viewed it as morally acceptable; 30 percent viewed it as morally wrong.
- In 2006, 61 percent viewed it as morally acceptable; 30 percent viewed it as morally wrong.
- In 2005, 60 percent viewed it as morally acceptable; 33 percent viewed it as morally wrong.
- In 2004, 54 percent viewed it as morally acceptable; 37 percent viewed it as morally wrong.
- In 2003, 54 percent viewed it as morally acceptable; 38 percent viewed it as morally wrong.
- In 2002, 52 percent viewed it as morally acceptable; 39 percent viewed it as morally wrong.

A 2009 Gallup poll found the following about opinions of stem cell research:

- 57 percent think medical research using stem cells obtained from human embryos is morally acceptable; 36 percent think it is morally wrong.

- Americans as a group thought medical research using embryonic stem cells was more moral than having a baby outside of marriage (51 percent); gay and lesbian relations (49 percent); doctor-assisted suicide (39 percent); abortion (36 percent); cloning animals (34 percent); suicide (15 percent); cloning humans (9 percent); polygamy (7 percent); and married people having an affair (7 percent).
- Americans as a group thought medical research using embryonic stem cells was less moral than divorce (62 percent said this was morally acceptable), the death penalty (62 percent), buying and wearing clothing made from animal fur (61 percent), and gambling (58 percent).

A September 2010 Harris Interactive/HealthDay poll found the following about American opinions of stem cell research:
- 58 percent of Republicans think stem cell research is morally acceptable.
- 69 percent of Catholics think stem cell research is morally acceptable.
- 58 percent of born-again Christians think stem cell research is morally acceptable.
- Two in three people said that if most scientists think embryonic stem cell research will lead to cures or the ability to prevent serious disease, they should be trusted to proceed with research.
- 20 percent think embryonic stem cell research comes too close to letting scientists "play God."
- 62 percent disagreed that embryonic stem cell research should be forbidden because it is immoral.

The Government's Role in Stem Cell Research
A 2010 CNN/Opinion Research Corporation poll found the following about stem cell research:
- 55 percent of Americans think the government should fund research that uses stem cells derived from human embryos.
- 41 percent of Americans think the government should not fund research that uses stem cells derived from human embryos.
- 4 percent are unsure.

- 70 percent of Democrats think the government should fund this research.
- 51 percent of Independents think the government should fund this research.
- 40 percent of Republicans think the government should fund this research.

A 2009 Gallup poll found the following about opinions of stem cell research:
- 14 percent of Americans think the government should place no restrictions on stem cell research.
- 38 percent think the government should ease restrictions on stem cell research.
- 22 percent think the government should keep current restrictions on stem cell research.
- 19 percent think the government should not fund stem cell research at all.
- 7 percent are unsure.

A 2009 CNN/Opinion Research Corporation poll found the following:
- 40 percent of Americans said it was moderately important to them that the president and Congress deal with the issue of stem cell research in the following year.
- 17 percent said it was extremely important.
- 16 percent said it was very important.
- 25 percent said it was not important.
- 2 percent were unsure.

A September 2010 Harris Interactive/HealthDay poll found the following about American opinions of stem cell research:
- 72 percent believe that scientists should be allowed to research on embryonic stem cells derived from embryos left over from in vitro fertilization procedures.
- 73 percent think stem cell research on such embryos should be allowed as long as the parents of the embryo give their permission, and the embryo would be destroyed if not used for research.

- 12 percent oppose any use of embryonic stem cells for research.
- A little more than 50 percent of respondents worried that if the government did not fund stem cell research, the United States would fall behind other nations in terms of developing new drugs and technologies to prevent disease.
- 28 percent said they did not think the interests of medical science should be put ahead of the preservation of human life, embryos included.

Glossary

blastocyst: An embryo that is just days old and is made up of between 150 and 200 cells. Blastocysts feature an inner cell mass, where embryonic stem cells are located. They also have an outer layer of cells called the trophoblast that will eventually form a placenta.

cell line: Cells that can be grown over time in a petri dish in a laboratory.

cloning: The process of creating genetically identical cells. Reproductive cloning is when genetically identical animals are made, such as Dolly the sheep. Therapeutic cloning (or somatic cell nuclear transfer [SCNT]) is when cells are replicated for therapeutic purposes. For example, SCNT might be used to create multiple cells that will not be rejected by a donor's immune system.

differentiation: When cells develop to become more complex and have a specialized function, such as liver cells or heart cells.

embryo: A group of cells that form after a sperm fertilizes an egg. The embryonic stage ends after eight weeks of gestation.

embryonic stem cell: Cells derived from the inner cell mass of a developing blastocyst. These cells can replicate themselves and can form all other cell types found in the body (a characteristic known as pluripotency).

induced pluripotent stem (iPS) cell: These stem cells are engineered from nonpluripotent cells (specialized cells, such as skin cells) and reprogrammed to become pluripotent, so that they mimic the undifferentiated state of embryonic stem cells.

in vitro fertilization (IVF): When eggs and sperm are united in a petri dish outside the body, which results in fertilized eggs. After a fertilized egg has divided over the course of several days, it is then implanted in a woman's body, where pregnancy will take place. IVF usually creates multiple fertilized eggs, many of which are discarded or frozen, since only one or two fertilized eggs are desired for a pregnancy.

multipotent stem cells: These stem cells can give rise to several different kinds of specialized cells or organs but not as many as pluripotent stem cells can. For example, multipotent blood stem cells can give rise to different kinds of blood cells, but not to the cells that make up other organs, such as the brain or liver.

pluripotent stem cells: Cells that can give rise to all other cell types found in the body, like embryonic stem cells.

somatic cell nuclear transfer (SCNT): Also called therapeutic cloning, this is when a nucleus of a cell (such as a skin cell) is put into an unfertilized egg, the nucleus of which has been removed. This creates an embryo that is allowed to develop to the blastocyst stage so researchers can harvest embryonic stem cells.

stem cells: Cells that can renew themselves and differentiate into specialized cells. Stem cells have a wide range of potential for differentiation. Embryonic stem cells (ES) can turn into any other cell in the body; adult stem cells (from mature, developed, or differentiated cells like skin) are less versatile; induced pluripotent stem cells fall in between.

tissue-specific stem cells (adult, or somatic, stem cells): These cells are found in different tissues of the body. They are multipotent, meaning they can give rise to some or all of the mature cell types found within the particular tissue or organ from which they came, but not others. For example, blood stem cells can give rise to all the cells that make up the blood but not the cells of other tissues.

undifferentiated cell: A cell that has not yet developed into a specialized cell type, such as a liver cell or blood cell. Embryonic stem cells are undifferentiated; skin cells are differentiated.

Organizations to Contact

The editors have compiled the following list of organizations concerned with the issues debated in this book. The descriptions are derived from materials provided by the organizations. All have publications or information available for interested readers. The list was compiled on the date of publication of the present volume; the information provided here may change. Be aware that many organizations take several weeks or longer to respond to inquiries, so allow as much time as possible for the receipt of requested materials.

American Association for the Advancement of Science (AAAS)
1200 New York Ave. NW
Washington, DC 20005
(202) 326-6400
e-mail: webmaster@aaas.org
website: www.aaas.org

AAAS, an international nonprofit organization, serves as an educator, leader, spokesperson, and professional association dedicated to advancing science around the world. It publishes the journal *Science,* as well as many scientific newsletters, books, and reports. A search of "stem cell research" on its website yields numerous articles and publications. AAAS also has an educational program that provides students with volunteer opportunities to learn more about what's happening in the world of science and to meet scientists and researchers working in a given field.

American Life League (ALL)
PO Box 1350
Stafford, VA 22555
(540) 659-4171 • fax: (540) 659-2586
e-mail: info@all.org
website: www.all.org

ALL is an educational pro-life organization that opposes abortion, artificial contraception, reproductive technologies, and fetal experimentation. It asserts that it is immoral to perform experiments on living human embryos and fetuses, whether inside or outside of the mother's womb. Its publications include the brochures *Stem Cell Research: The Science of Human Sacrifice* and *Human Cloning: The Science of Deception.*

American Medical Association (AMA)
515 N. State St.
Chicago, IL 60654
(800) 621-83350
website: www.ama-assn.org

The AMA is the largest professional association for medical doctors. It helps set standards for medical education and practices, and it is a powerful lobby in Washington for physicians' interests. The association publishes an e-newsletter as well as journals for many medical fields, including the weekly *Journal of the American Medical Association (JAMA).* In addition, searching for "stem cells" on its website retrieves numerous articles about stem cell research.

The Center for Bioethics & Human Dignity (CBHD)
2065 Half Day Rd.
Deerfield, IL 60015
(847) 317-8180 • fax: (847) 317-8101
e-mail: info@cbhd.org
website: www.cbhd.org

Formed in 1994 by Christian bioethicists, CBHD is a nonprofit international organization that strives to provide research, publications, and teaching to engage leaders in bioethics. The center has initiated a number of projects, including *Do No Harm: The Coalition of Americans for Research Ethics,* a partnership of researchers, bioethicists, academics, and others that serves as an information clearinghouse on the ethics and science of stem cell research. CBHD maintains the Do No Harm website, which advocates for adult stem cell research and other medical technologies that do not involve the destruction of human embryos.

Center for Genetics and Society
1936 University Ave., Ste. 350
Berkeley, CA 94704
(510) 625-0819

e-mail: info@geneticsandsociety.org
website: www.geneticsandsociety.org

This nonprofit information and public affairs organization works to encourage responsible uses and effective societal governance of the rapidly advancing human genetic and reproductive technologies, including stem cell research.

Christian Coalition of America
PO Box 37030, Washington, DC 20013-7030
(202) 479-6900
website: www.cc.org

The Christian Coalition of America is a conservative grassroots political organization that offers Christians a vehicle to become actively involved in shaping their local and national governments. It represents a pro-family agenda and works to educate America about critical issues, including opposing the destruction of human embryos through stem cell research. Its website provides action alerts, a weekly newsletter, commentary, and voter education information that encourages citizens to vote.

Coalition for the Advancement of Medical Research (CAMR)
750 Seventeenth St. NW, Ste. 1100
Washington, DC 20006
(202) 725-0339
e-mail:camresearch@yahoo.com
website: www.camradvocacy.org

CAMR is a bipartisan coalition, composed of more than a hundred nationally recognized patient organizations, universities, scientific societies, and foundations. CAMR focuses on developing better treatments and cures for individuals with life-threatening illnesses and disorders. It periodically takes polls to gauge Americans' response to stem cell research, and its website provides links to the publications reporting on the most recent developments and events related to stem cell research.

Concerned Women for America (CWA)
1015 Fifteenth St. NW, Ste. 1100
Washington, DC 20005
(202) 488-7000
website: www.cwfa.org

The CWA is a women's public policy organization that aims to bring the principles of the Bible into all levels of public policy. CWA focuses on preserving traditional family values as well as protecting the sanctity of human life. Its website has article links, press releases, and legislative alerts.

Council for Responsible Genetics (CRG)
5 Upland Rd., Ste. 3
Cambridge, MA 02140
(617) 868-0870
e-mail: crg@gene-watch.org
website: www.gene-watch.org

CRG is a national nonprofit, nongovernmental organization of scientists, health professionals, trade unionists, women's health activists, and others who work to ensure that genetic technologies are developed safely and in the best interest of the public. The council publishes the bimonthly newsletter *GeneWatch* and has several programs that address specific genetics-related issues, including a program called Human Genetic Manipulation and Cloning.

Family Research Council (FRC)
801 G St. NW
Washington, DC 20001
(202) 393-2100
website: www.frc.org

The FRC is a Christian nonprofit think tank and lobbying organization that promotes the traditional family unit based on Judeo-Christian values. It advocates for national policies that protect traditional notions of marriage and family and the sanctity of human life. One of its central focuses is on human life and bioethics, and it opposes research that harms, manipulates, or destroys an embryonic human being and vigorously supports adult stem cell therapies that can treat patients.

Genetics Policy Institute (GPI)
11924 Forest Hill Blvd., Ste. 22
Wellington, FL 33414
(888) 238-1423
website: www.genpol.org

The GPI is the leading nonprofit organization dedicated to establishing a positive legal framework to advance stem cell research. GPI maintains science and legal advisory boards composed of leading stem cell researchers, disease experts, ethicists, and legal experts and a dedicated full-time staff of policy experts that are available to educate the public and media on stem cell issues.

Harvard Stem Cell Institute (HSCI)
42 Church St.
Cambridge, MA 02138
(617) 496-4050
e-mail: hsci@harvard.edu
website: www.hsci.harvard.edu

The HSCI, composed of Harvard Medical School and eighteen hospitals and research institutions, hosts one of the largest concentrations of biomedical researchers in the world. Its publication *Stem Cell Lines* is published three times per year and its monthly newsletter publishes the scientific work of its faculty. The institute offers scientific overviews that focus on the use of stem cells and potential therapeutic applications.

The Hastings Center
21 Malcolm Gordon Rd.
Garrison, NY 10524-4125
(845) 424-4040
e-mail: mail@thehastingscenter.org
website: www.thehastingscenter.org

The Hastings Center is an independent nonpartisan and nonprofit bioethics research institute. Since its founding in 1969, the center has played a central role in responding to advances in medicine, the biological sciences, and the social sciences by raising ethical questions related to such advances, including stem cell research. The center publishes books, papers, guidelines, and the bimonthly *Hastings Center Report*.

Institute for Stem Cell Research (ISCR)
School of Biological Sciences
University of Edinburgh
W. Mains Rd.

Edinburgh, Scotland EH9 3JQ
+44 (0) 131 650 5828
e-mail: p.hope@ed.ac.uk
website: www.iscr.ed.ac.uk

The ISCR is a global stem cell research and technology center devoted to developing stem cell therapies that can be used to treat human injury and disease. The center hosts state-of-the-art research and laboratory facilities to accommodate research in stem cell culture and experimental embryology. ISCR also offers regular seminar series, and its website provides links to many institutes doing stem cell research internationally.

International Society for Stem Cell Research (ISSCR)
111 Deer Lake Rd., Ste. 100
Deerfield, IL 60015
(847) 509-1944
e-mail: isscr@isscr.org
website: www.isscr.org

Formed in 2002, the ISSCR is an independent, nonprofit organization created to foster the exchange of information on stem cell research. It publishes a monthly newsletter called the *Pulse,* which provides the latest stem cell research news, schedules of scientific and industry meetings, and other general information useful to scientists working with stem cells. ISSCR is also affiliated with the award-winning journal *Cell Stem Cell,* a forum that covers a wide range of information about stem cell biology research.

The Michael J. Fox Foundation for Parkinson's Research
PO Box 780, Church Street Station
New York, NY 10008-078
website: www.michaeljfox.org

This organization is headed by Michael J. Fox, a prominent face in the fight to support stem cell research. Fox was a popular actor when in 1991 he was diagnosed with Parkinson's disease, a degenerative and debilitating neural condition. The foundation lobbies for federal support of embryonic stem cell research because it believes that that research is most promising to cure Parkinson's and similar diseases.

Stem Cell Information
Office of Communications and Public Liaison
National Institutes of Health
1 Center Dr., MSC 0188
Bethesda, MD 20892-0199
(301) 496-5787
e-mail: stemcell@mail.nih.gov
website: http://stemcells.nih.gov

Stem Cell Information is the National Institutes of Health's resource for stem cell research. It provides the latest information on important stem cell research topics, as well as current federal policy information. Its website provides basic stem cell information, stem cell reports that review the state of research, a glossary, photos and illustrations, and links to related sources.

Stem Cell Network
501 Smyth Rd., Rm. CCW-6189
Ottawa, ON K1H 8L6 Canada
(613) 739-6675
e-mail: info@stemcellnetwork.com
website: www.stemcellnetwork.ca

This Canadian organization supports cutting-edge projects that lead to the development of new and better treatments for millions of patients in Canada and around the world. The network works with more than a hundred scientists, clinicians, engineers, and social scientists.

For Further Reading

Books

Bush, George W. *Decision Points.* New York: Crown, 2010. The former president explains how he arrived at his decisions on many controversial subjects, including stem cell research. A full chapter is devoted to his opinions on stem cell research and how his eight years in office affected that rapidly changing field.

Drapeau, Christian. *Cracking the Stem Cell Code.* Portland, OR: Sutton Hart, 2010. This book discusses the potential of adult stem cells and considers the future of this cutting-edge industry.

Herold, Eve. *Stem Cell Wars: Inside Stories from the Frontlines.* New York: Palgrave Macmillan, 2007. This book argues that it is the moral responsibility of the government to support stem cell research in order to provide treatments and cures for conditions afflicting millions of people.

Park, Alice. *The Stem Cell Hope: How Stem Cell Medicine Can Change Our Lives.* New York: Hudson Street, 2011. This accessible book, written for the general reader, explains how the stem cell debate has changed to move beyond embryonic stem cells.

Perry, Yvonne. *Right to Recover: Winning the Political and Religious Wars over Stem Cell Research in America.* Mequon, WI: Nightengale, 2007. A well-researched book that reveals the many ways in which Americans view embryonic stem cell research.

Peters, Ted. *Sacred Cells? Why Christians Should Support Stem Cell Research.* Lanham, MD: Rowman & Littlefield, 2010. This book tells the story of three Christian theologians in favor of stem cell research.

Scott, Christopher Thomas. *Stem Cell Now: A Brief Introduction to the Coming Medical Revolution.* New York: Plume, 2006. An accessible book that takes a neutral look at the basics of stem cell research and the political, medical, and religious controversies that surround it.

Periodicals and Internet Sources

American Catholic. "A Pro-Life Future for Stem Cell Research?," January 26, 2010. http://the-american-catholic.com/2010/01/26/a-pro-life-future-for-stem-cell-research/.

Center for American Progress. "Eight Reasons to Applaud Action on Stem Cells," March 2009. www.americanprogress.org/issues/2009/03/stem_cell_action.html.

Daley, George. "iPS Cells: A Promising New Platform for Drug Discovery," *Vector,* Children's Hospital Boston, September 23, 2010. http://vectorblog.org/2010/09/ips-cells-a-promising-new-platform-for-drug-discovery/.

Discover 80 Beats (blog). "The Trouble with Lab-Created Stem Cells—and Why They Won't Displace Embryonic Ones," February 16, 2010. http://blogs.discovermagazine.com/80beats/2010/02/16/the-trouble-with-adult-stem-cells—and-why-they-wont-displace-embryonic-ones/.

Ethics Committee of the American Society for Reproductive Medicine, "Donating Spare Embryos for Stem Cell Research," *Fertility and Sterility,* March 2009. www.sart.org/uploadedFiles/ASRM_Content/News_and_Publications/Ethics_Committee_Reports_and_Statements/donatingspare.pdf.

Flynn, Raymond L. "A True Story About a Little Boy," *Boston Globe,* November 14, 2010. www.boston.com/bostonglobe/editorial_opinion/oped/articles/2010/11/14/a_true_story_about_a_little_boy/.

George, Robert P., and Eric Cohen. "The President Politicizes Stem Cell Research," *Wall Street Journal,* March 10, 2009. http://online.wsj.com/article/SB123664280083277765.html.

Hirschfield, Brad. "Resistance to Stem Cell Research About Fear, Not Faith," *Washington Post,* March 10, 2009. http://newsweek.washingtonpost.com/onfaith/panelists/brad_hirschfield/2009/03/fear_not_faith_guides_most_resistance_to_stem_cell_research.html.

Jacoby, Susan. "A 'Slippery Slope' Only if We're Stupid," *Washington Post,* March 10, 2009. http://newsweek.washingtonpost.com/onfaith/panelists/susan_jacoby/2009/03/embryonic_stem_cell_research_a.html.

Keiper, Adam, and Yuval Levin. "Stem Cells, Life, and the Law," *National Review,* August 25, 2010. www.nationalreview.com/articles /244637/stem-cells-life-and-law-adam-keiper?pg=1.

Knox, Richard. "Offshore Stem Cell Clinics Sell Hope, Not Science," National Public Radio, July 26, 2010. www.npr.org/templates /story/story.php?storyId=128696529.

Krauthammer, Charles. "President Obama and Stem Cells—Science Fiction," *Washington Post,* March 12, 2009. www.washingtonpost .com/wp-dyn/content/article/2009/03/12/AR2009031202764 .html.

McEwan, Robert. "These Cures Are No Longer Science Fiction," *Globe & Mail* (Toronto), June 16, 2011. www.theglobeandmail .com/news/opinions/opinion/these-cures-are-no-longer-science -fiction/article2062110/.

Merrill, Jacqueline Pfeffer. "Embryos in Limbo," *New Atlantis,* Spring 2009. www.thenewatlantis.com/publications/embryos-in-limbo.

New York Times. "Sense on the Stem Cell Front," May 3, 2011. www .nytimes.com/2011/05/03/opinion/03tue2.html.

New York Times. "Wrong Direction on Stem Cells," August 25, 2010. www.nytimes.com/2010/08/25/opinion/25wed1.html ?_r=1&ref=opinion.

Rattani, Abbas. "Scientific Research, Revolution and Bioethics," *Berman Institute Bioethics Bulletin*, March 16, 2011. http://bioethics bulletin.org/archive/scientific-research-revolution-and-bioethics/.

Riggan, Kirsten. "An Update on the Frontlines of Alternatives to Embryonic Stem Cell Research," Center for Bioethics & Human Dignity, May 6, 2011. http://cbhd.org/content/update-frontlines -alternatives-embryonic-stem-cell-research.

Rugnetta, Michael. "A New Debate Can't Wait," *Huffington Post*, March 9, 2009. www.huffingtonpost.com/michael-rugnetta/a-new -debate-cant-wait_b_173281.html.

Sahlman, William A. "Hobbling Science and Scientists," *Boston Globe,* September 19, 2010. www.boston.eom/bostonglobe/editorial _opinion/oped/articles/2010/09/19/hobbling_science_and_scien tists/.

Schwager, Clare. "Snowflake Babies Bring New Angle to Stem Cell Debate," *Iowa State Daily,* March 30, 2011. www.iowastatedaily .com/article_2ee4aef8-5928-11e0-b9d6-001cc4c03286.html.

Singh, Seema. "The Rebirth of Stem Cells," *Forbes,* September 26, 2011. www.forbes.com/2011/09/26/forbes-india-rebirth-stem -cells-stephen-minger.html.

Vergano, Dan. "Stem Cell Alternatives Show Early Aging Abnormalities," *USA Today,* February 12, 2010. http://content.usa today.com/communities/sciencefair/post/2010/02/stem-cell-alter natives-show-early-aging-abnormalities/1.

Wagner, John E. "Stem Cells, Cloning and the GOP," *Minneapolis Star Tribune,* April 9, 2011. www.startribune.com/opinion/other views/119438024.html.

Washington Times. "'Snowflake' Baby Stars Opposite Obama," March 10, 2009. www.washingtontimes.com/news/2009/mar/10 /snowflake-baby-stars-opposite-obama/?page=all.

Websites

Closer Look (www.closerlookatstemcells.org). This site, maintained by the International Society for Stem Cell Research, arms patients with information regarding what is possible, and what is not possible, for stem cell treatments. The society's goal is to prevent people from being taken advantage of by overseas clinics.

NOVA's **Stem Cell Research Page** (www.pbs.org/wgbh/nova/body /stem-cells-research.html). This information page features articles, videos, blogs, and multimedia that explores various aspects of stem cell science.

Stem Cell Action Network (www.stemcellaction.org/). A grassroots volunteer advocacy group composed of patients and their families and friends that supports the funding of stem cell research. It works with America's scientific and medical organizations in the hope of finding cures for many medical conditions, including Parkinson's, Alzheimer's, juvenile diabetes, and even spinal cord injury. Members petition, educate, and vote to advance support for embryonic stem cell research.

Stem Cell Science Edition (www.stemcellresources.org). This site, maintained by the BioScience Network, features breaking news and other articles relating to stem cell research. A multimedia section features videos and other animation that helps students grasp difficult concepts.

Student Society for Stem Cell Research (www.ssscr.org). This international network is dedicated to the advancement of scientific research for cures. Its website contains information on how to start a Student Society for Stem Cell Research (SSSCR) chapter at a high school or college.

Index

Picture Credits

© 3D4Medical/Photo Researchers, Inc., 13

© AP Images/Haraz Ghanbari, 37

© AP Images/Gerald Herbert, 66

© AP Images/Brennan Linsley, 78

© AP Images/Paul Sakuma, 71

© AP Images/Reed Saxon, 88

© Brian Bell/Photo Researchers, Inc., 34

Gale/Cengage Learning, 15, 19, 32, 38, 43, 52, 57, 77, 84, 90, 95, 96, 102

© Ken Cedeno/Bloomberg via Getty Images, 21

© HO/Reuters/Landov, 101

© Laguna Design/Photo Researchers, Inc., 31

© David McNew/Getty Images, 10

© Javier Rojas/PI/Landov, 83

© Chip Somodevilla/Getty Images, 94

© Pasquale Sorrentino/Photo Researchers, Inc., 50

© SPL/Photo Researchers, Inc., 46

© Volker Steger/Photo Researchers, Inc., 59

© Shawn Thew/Getty Images, 74

© Geoff Thompkinson/Photo Researchers, Inc., 25